Chrysalis:

Angels, ETs & Us

Mark Kimmel

Chrysalis:
Angels, ETs & Us

Mark Kimmel

www.cosmicparadigm.com

Paradigm Books
PO Box 3568
Pagosa Springs, Colorado
88@paradigmbooks.org

ISBN 978-0-9720151-5-8

Who are you?

Why are you here?

Do not underestimate your importance.

Earth Star

Everything was so different, so strange. I looked at my feet. I wore no shoes. My feet floated, barely touching the surface. The surface itself was so beautiful, multi-colored, multi-hued, and with colors I had never seen before. How could I describe colors I had never seen before?

Raising my eyes a little, I saw my surroundings. What appeared to be bushes were likewise of brilliant colors and hues that reflected my emotions. They shimmered as if they were alive. They were far from solid, more like a mist, but yet there was form to them.

I looked at my hands. They were still my hands but they were younger, no wrinkles or scars. My hands were beautiful. I reached out to touch a bush. My hand floated within its branches and leaves, as if I were a part of the bush yet somehow separate.

Glancing upward I saw a brilliant violet sky. Yes there were white clouds, but they seemed so low as to be just beyond my reach. I discovered that I was taller. I could see over low bushes; my head was aligned with distant trees. Oh, and the trees. They too were of brilliant new colors as if fall had arrived with its beauty, but many times more brilliant and once again intense new colors.

I took a step forward. I seemed to float on the surface of what I deemed to be a path. Tentatively I set one foot in front of another. The surface was soft to each step. I felt as if I was one with the path, one with the bushes, the trees, and the sky.

I had no concern for myself. I felt enveloped by this wondrous beauty. I felt very much at peace; nothing worried me, I was in no hurry. All I wanted was to be a part of this grand display. I was in form, yet was not in my old body.

I was in a higher vibration, beyond my old physical form. Not only beyond form, but beyond my old ways of being.

Looking ahead on the path, I spied a tall thin figure coming toward me. She had impossibly thin arms and legs, and a face like none of Earth. As she approached I felt her warmth and friendliness. My heart flooded with love, for I knew beyond a doubt that she was a sister. When we embraced, I felt light and love flow between us. Then I knew for sure, I was on the 5th Dimension Earth, and that the Earth Star now shined for all in the universe.

To Jim Self, Joan Walker, Archangels
and Ascended Masters,
particularly Archangel Michael,
and the Andromedans
who have enabled me to experience
the non-physical and discover who I really am.

Chrysalis

Index

Chrysalis

Introduction

Extraterrestrials and Ultraterrestrials

Do you know who you really are? Do you know why you are here? Do you truly understand the physical and non-physical context in which you live? In the following pages we will answer these questions, and more; for the answers give new meaning to our lives. In this book I, along with others, will reveal the vastness and grandeur of creation: the universes and the beings therein; and we will point the way for you to realize how important you are in this grand scheme of everything.

This book is based on my interactions with extraterrestrials, Archangels, and Ultraterrestrials without their invaluable participation, and the experiences through which they have led me, this book would not be. I am particularly indebted to Archangel Michael for his encouragement and assistance, and to my Andromedan brothers and sisters. Some of the words herein are my transcriptions of communications received from them, plus my personal experiences with them. Herein you will find differing points of view, accounts, and opinions, including my own.

This book presents a snapshot of what was revealed, believed and experienced as of the 21st Century of "Western Civilization" of Earth. If these were presented in a different era or planetary tradition, the words used would be much different.

I use the word, "extraterrestrials," to refer to beings in physical form from this universe, regardless of the type of physical form. I use "Ultraterrestrials" to refer to a collective of beings of non-physical form and non-form, including Archangels,

Ascended Masters and others of whom I have no knowledge, both in this universe and throughout other universes, all of whom are closely allied with Source.

I have undergone an amazing personal transformation to a state of consciousness of which I had never dreamed. I am very happy in this place. Based on communications from Archangels and extraterrestrials, I now believe much differently about the creation of Earth and what the rest of the universe is about. Based on my experiences in the non-physical, I now have a better understanding of who I am and why I am here. Based on communications from non-physical beings and from extraterrestrials, I believe that I have a good understanding of where Earth and her human civilization are headed.

More specifically, I have moved from a perspective wherein I believed that life on Earth was all there was, to belief about life on other planets, to seeing indisputable evidence of off-planet beings, to telepathic communications with extraterrestrials, to communications with Ultraterrestrials, and to having experiences in the non-physical as well as creating therein. This journey has expanded my perspective from Earth, to the cosmic, to the non-physical, to the Divine.

Without diminishing their importance to my journey, I have abandoned many of my former beliefs, but not the knowing I have acquired along the way. In this book I delineate where I now see myself and Earth in contrast to where I used to see myself. I show that this understanding leads to greater comprehension of the larger reality. By doing so, I hope to encourage you to take steps to find out more about who you really are. And once you discover that, discover why you are here. I see my fellow Earth humans and myself in a chrysalis state of being: We are just about ready to emerge as butterflies in a wondrous new Earth.

In my writing and speaking I delineate between what I *know* or what I *understand* to be true from my experiences and/or an inner knowingness and what I *believe* to be true because I respect the source of that information, both physical beings and non-physical. I will follow that practice in this book, but make it more specific to designate whether it is a human source of my beliefs, or whether the beliefs are based on communications with off-planet beings, or whether it is a knowing based on communications with beings of the non-physical. I will also designate as reports or accounts those things and events that have been told to me by other humans. I am sure you will see contrasts among these points-of-view.

In the pages that follow, I share much of what I have learned over the years about the larger reality, most of which is based on experiences and the knowing derived therefrom. I hope you will find it as interesting, valuable and exciting as I have.

April 2015
Mark Kimmel

NOTE: Throughout this book, words that are in *italics* at the end of chapters indicate that they are communications from a group of Ultraterrestrials known to me as *"The One."* They began to communicate in the summer of 2014, when I first undertook to write this book. I believe you will find the contrast between their much broader perspective and my more limited view to be most enlightening. I am most grateful for their assistance.

We are "The One" — a group of Ultraterrestrials. Our role is that of observers. We are here to assist Mark in the presentation of this material. We welcome you and trust that the following will uplift your individual energies for the benefit of all in this universe. We will make additional comments throughout this book. Know that you are engaged in a wondrous event: The rebirth of the physical universe to a higher consciousness. Welcome to this marvelous undertaking.

Chrysalis

1

UFOs and Extraterrestrials

It began on May 11, 2001, as I watched in utter fascination. The twenty-two witnesses of the Disclosure Project stood before the prestigious National Press Club in Washington, D.C. and revealed their experiences with unmistakable sightings of extra-terrestrial craft. They talked about their experiences with retrieving the bodies of beings not of this planet. And they spoke of the cover-up by the government and military contractors, and of the reverse engineering of technology recovered from downed extra-terrestrial craft. Amazed, I watched as the camera panned a room full of television cameras and reporters. At the conclusion of this extraordinary event, I truly believed that there were extraterrestrials and they were here on Earth. None of the four hours of this extraordinary testimony by government officials, corporate contractors, and knowledgeable private citizens found its way into the mainstream media.

The end of June that same year, I went into the Baca Grande, a semi-desert area near Crestone, Colorado, to the west of the Sangre de Cristo Mountains. We were just north of the Great San Dunes National Park. There were forty of us that first night, men and women from all walks of life, all were eager to see a UFO. We sat on folding chairs, in a circle so we could scan the night sky in every direction; we all were eager to become ambassadors to the universe under the auspices of Dr. Steven Greer of CSETI (The Center for the Study of Extraterrestrial Intelligence).

My first sighting was of a ship that Dr. Greer dubbed as "Kindness." It was several times brighter than any star. Excited, I watched my first UFO linger for a moment, then corkscrew out of the atmosphere.

A while later that same night, I was called to look toward my left. There I saw four yellow squares suspended against the dark mountains of the Sangre de Cristo. They appeared to be the lights of a passenger train; three were wide open, the fourth only half. I could not tell whether they were far away or close by. I watched until they blinked out. By the end of that first night, I was shaking from head to toe — it was a combination of excitement and fear.

Later that night, blinking lights approached the group, coming from the side of Blanca Peak. Then the lights faded away. I asked Dr. Greer about them, because many in the group had seen the lights. I was told that the ET craft had sensed that too many people in the group were frightened and not ready for contact. I had no doubts that what we had seen that night were not from this world.

Another night that same week, we were in our vehicles in a parking lot near Zapata Falls on the side of Blanca Peak, over-looking the dunes at the national park. It was raining with thunder and lightning, so no sitting outside. After a couple of hours of looking around and chatting with the others in the car, I was called to look right. Yelling, "Look, look," I pointed out the side window at brilliant blue lights. A hundred yards away I saw a craft materialize out of the sheer cliff of the mountain. No, the mountain did not open to expose a doorway; the ship just emerged. I will never forget the intense blue lights of the craft as it sped out over the valley and disappeared into the atmosphere. Two of the three others in the car also saw the craft. By the end of the week, and all my experiences, I knew for sure that there were extraterrestrials and that they were here.

A year later with a CSETI group in the same area, in a similar circle of thirty people, I watched three ET craft settle in a location that appeared to be near the full moon in the western sky. They were each about 5 to 10 percent the size of the moon and individually as bright. It was hard to tell how far away they were, or whether they were even in Earth's atmosphere. Not long after, two military jets screamed overhead, aiming toward the three ships. After a moment, the ET ships winked out.

Another time, I was seated with another CSETI group and felt my chair bounce, as if someone had bumped it. I looked around; no one was behind me. A few minutes later, others in the circle reported the same experience. That night we did not see any phenomenon, but my bump under the chair was enough to convince me that my extraterrestrial friends were present.

My experiences with CSETI plus other sighting of ET craft have left me with a knowing: There is extraterrestrial life and it is here. I never felt threatened by any of my experiences. I came to learn that the energy I was putting out was being reflected by benevolent phenomenon.

After my first week with CSETI, I came home to *Trillion,* the book I had been writing since 1997, when it spilled out of my computer, as I was writing an academic paper. It was all about a group of very human-like extraterrestrials who were among us. I had paid two very experienced editors to go through the book, they had made their changes, and I had started my own publishing company to publish the book because I was told that, "No one in New York will touch this." Based on my CSETI experiences, I made a single change to *Trillion*. I now knew how extraterrestrials traveled faster than the speed of light: They dematerialized.

In the three books of the *Paradigm Trilogy, Trillion, Decimal* and *One*, I portrayed the experiences of human-like extraterrestrials walking the Earth and interacting with ordinary humans. These three books are available at my web site, www.cosmicparadigm.com, and at www.Amazon.com. In addition, I have made many presentations in connection with marketing these books; some of these are available at www.YouTube.com.

In the *Paradigm Trilogy* I wrote from an extraterrestrial point-of-view, and from a 4th Dimension perspective. I now know that I was assisted in these perspectives from off-planet sources during the writing of these books. I translated their communications, colored by my beliefs at that time, into the resulting stories in these books. I portrayed Sarah, the heroine of the *Paradigm Trilogy*, with a very human-like body in most respects. I now see that my earlier portrayals were a blend of my imagination with the assistance I was receiving, but colored by my underdeveloped ability to receive telepathic communications. Only now am I comprehending that these books are somewhat autobiographical, for I now know that I am a soul who has spent many lifetimes on planets in the Andromeda Galaxy, and one who is now incarnated in the body of an Earth human.

I now understand that Earth humans are unique, and I believe that beings from other planets are similarly unique. Beings of other planets range from the very spiritual to those with a less developed consciousness, and from highly technological to primitive. I know that beings from other planets are real because I have seen their starships and have experienced other phenomenon beyond conventional and/or scientific explanation, things that can only be attributed to off-planet beings.

What follows in this chapter is not meant to be an exhaustive disclosure of all that relates to extraterrestrials, for that would take many books. I will first highlight events that make the case for off-planet beings interacting with us.

Battle of Los Angeles

I begin with this event because it occurred long before the Internet and digital photography. According to reports in the *Los Angeles Times*, on Wednesday, February 25, 1942, an unidentified craft hovered over the city of Los Angeles. This event, dubbed the "Battle of Los Angeles," was witnessed by hundreds of thousands of residents of the area. Spotlights, intent on spotting Japanese aircraft, played over the motionless craft. The military lobbed almost 2,000 rounds of high explosive shells at the floating sphere. Unscathed, the hovering UFO leisurely moved off to the south and disappeared over the ocean south of Long Beach. Six civilians were killed, others injured — the results of exploding shells' fragments as the military battled the craft. Reports of this event were not published beyond Los Angeles and were lost to the general public amidst other news about WWII.

Roswell, New Mexico

No discussion of UFOs and extraterrestrials would be complete without some mention of Roswell. It is the most thoroughly investigated incident of its kind. Below is a brief summary.

On July 4, 1947, an unidentified flying object crashed on a ranch northwest of Roswell. Rancher W.W. "Mack" Brazel found debris from the crash, after a fierce thunderstorm the night before. Maj. Jesse Marcel, intelligence officer for the 509th Bomber Group, stationed at Roswell Army Air Field, was sent to investigate. Subsequently, the debris site was closed for several days while the military cleared the wreckage.

In later testimony Marcel said, "The debris was strewn over a wide area, I guess maybe three-quarters of a mile long and a few hundred feet wide." Scattered in the debris were small bits of metal. Along with the metal fragments were almost weightless I-beam-like structures that were three-eighths inch by one-quarter inch, that would neither bend nor break. Some of these I-beams had indecipherable characters along the length, in two colors. He also described metal debris the thickness of tinfoil that was indestructible. There were also reports of alien bodies that were recovered.

The authorities dismissed this event as the crash of a weather balloon. Nonetheless, several thousand people visit the International Research Center and Library in Roswell each year.

Project Blue Book

The U.S. Air Force undertook a study of UFOs about the time

of the Roswell incident. Project Blue Book began under the name Project Sign, evolved into Project Grudge, and then finally took the name Blue Book in 1952. After 22 years of official investigations of thousands of UFO reports, the project was terminated in 1969. Of the 12,618 sightings considered under Blue Book, 701 have remained "unidentified."

The final conclusions of Project Blue Book were:

1) No UFO reported, investigated and evaluated by the Air Force has ever given any indication of threat to national security.

2) There has been no evidence submitted to or discovered by the Air Force that sightings categorized as "unidentified" represent technological developments or principles beyond the range of present-day scientific knowledge.

3) There has been no evidence indicating that sightings categorized as "unidentified" are extraterrestrial vehicles.

COMMENT: I remember seeing a copy of the executive summary for Project Blue Book in 1964. It was labeled, "Top Secret." In it were amazing photos of "flying saucers." A few days later, I was back to being so enmeshed in the conventional paradigm and my career that I forgot all about it. I did not recall it until many years later, after my week with CSETI in the Baca Grande.

Eduard "Billy" Meier

He is best known for his collection of the clearest, most detailed photographs of ET craft that we have. He was invited by the Pleiadians to take pictures of their ET craft.

Contact with extraterrestrials began for Billy on Tuesday, January 28, 1975, 2:12 PM: A strange craft with visitors from the Pleiades landed in the field not far from his home in the Swiss countryside of Hinwel. In the ensuing four years, he would take 800 remarkable photos of Pleiadian crafts and record over 3,000 pages of notes on his conversations with them. In Chapter 4 of this book, you will find excerpts of these messages from the Pleiadians.

You may investigate Billy further at: billymeierufocase.com/

Belgium UFO Flap

Of all the reports of UFO sightings, some of the most intriguing ones are those that come in waves, have multiple witnesses, and photographs. One of the most heralded cases of this type was the Belgian flap that began in November of 1989. No less than thirty different groups of witnesses, and three separate groups of police officers documented the events of November 29. All of the reports related a large object flying at low altitude. The craft was of a flat, triangular shape, with lights underneath. This giant craft made not a sound as it slowly, fearlessly, moved across the landscape of Belgium. There was free sharing of information as the Belgian populace tracked this craft as it moved from the town of Liege to the border of the Netherlands and Germany.

This first startling sighting would evolve into a wave over the next several months. On two occasions, a pair of F-16 fighters chased the mysterious object, but to no avail. On March 30, 1990, a frantic call to military headquarters came from a Belgian national police captain. He marveled at a giant triangle passing over, and simultaneously two ground radar stations were reporting an object of unknown origin on their screens. One of these bases was NATO controlled near the city of Glons, southeast of Brussels. After contacting other radar facilities, they learned that at least four other stations were also reporting the object on their screens. The object was moving across their screens slowly, and failed to send a transponder signal to identify itself.

The extraordinary sightings continued for months as the triangular craft was witnessed more than 1,000 times, both day and night. The object dipped low enough to easily be seen with the naked eye, and the event became one of the biggest stories in the Belgian media. Another unusual occurrence associated with the

Belgian flap was the inability to take a clear photograph of it. Many observers had their cameras ready, and took what they thought would be clear images, but when the film was developed, the image was blurred, and the craft's outline was vague at best.

Rendlesham, U.K.

In 1980 two air bases owned by the RAF, namely R.A.F./ U.S.A.F Bentwaters and R.A.F./U.S.A.F Woodbridge, were leased to the U.S. Air Force and reputedly held the largest stockpile of tactical nuclear weapons in non-communist Europe. Woodbridge was also the home of the 67th Aerospace Rescue and Recovery Squadron — a unit that reported directly to the U.S. Department of Defense in Washington.

At approximately 2:00 AM on the 27th of December 1980, an unidentified object was picked up by radar at R.A.F. Watton in Norfolk (UK). The object went off the screen in the area of Rendlesham Forest in Suffolk. R.A.F./U.S.A.F Bentwaters also tracked the unidentified object.

At approximately 3:00 AM two U.S.A.F security guards observed unusual lights outside the back gate of R.A.F. Woodbridge and three patrolmen were sent to investigate. These three men reported seeing a strange glowing object seemingly of metallic appearance and of a triangular shape. They reported it being approximately 2 to 3 meters across the base and 2 meters tall, giving off a bright white light which illuminated the entire forest. Also, it had a pulsing red light on top and a bank of blue lights underneath. When the men approached the object, it maneuvered through the forest and out of view. It was later reported that the base commander, Colonel Gordon Williams, communicated directly with the occupants of the unidentified craft.

Lt. Colonel Charles Halt, Deputy Base Commander at Woodbridge, had insisted that the first night's events be entered in the security police log, but the second night's event tore him away from his dinner. Armed with a tape recorder, Lt. Colonel Halt and a number of other servicemen witnessed the events as they unfolded — a detailed tape recording being made.

A full report dated 13th January 1981 was sent to the British Ministry of Defense by Lt. Colonel Halt. The M.O.D.'s ultimate response was: "The department satisfied itself at the time that there was no reason to consider that the alleged sighting had any defense significance."

One of the military witnesses, Larry Warren (then 19), a U.S.A.F. Security Specialist, later became regarded as the "whistle blower" as far as the incidents at Rendlesham are concerned. His chilling first-hand account of what happened on the night of December 28, 1980 and how the Government covered up these incidents is presented in the book, *Left at East Gate*.

In Larry's own words: "As my mind tried to register what I was looking at, the ball of light exploded in a blinding flash. Shards of light and particles fell into the fog. Several cops ran into the woods. I couldn't move; I tried to cover my eyes, but it was too late. Why I didn't run, I don't know. But now, right in front of me was a machine occupying the spot where the fog had been."

Larry Warren was a member of the U.S.A.F. Security Police stationed at an American base on British soil. He was taken from his guard post to investigate strange lights in a forest clearing near the base. Here he and other enlisted men and officers confronted an alien craft on the ground. Even the base deputy commander came forward to verify some of the details of this case.

2014 UFO Sightings

Sightings of UFOs continue across the world. For the month of October 2014, MUFON (Mutual UFO Network) compiled 781 reported sightings of UFOs, with 642 from the United States. Due to the popularity and availability of YouTube, there are fewer words now days to explain these sightings. Following are references to some of these. With little effort you can find many others.

- https://www.youtube.com/watch?v=D_muaRfbE7A
- https://www.youtube.com/watch?v=hMPRBREySjo
- https://www.youtube.com/watch?v=S-wcntY0Olw

- https://www.youtube.com/watch?v=6tBpr9jzrEw
- https://www.youtube.com/watch?v=VKVbP1_umcQ
- https://www.youtube.com/watch?v=G9Hw7nCxvvg
- https://www.youtube.com/watch?v=suBp3ai-xG8

COMMENTS: We have few clear photos of ET craft because many of them exist at a different frequency than do we — as demonstrated in Belgium. The Air Force's Project Blue Book does have photos, and people like Col. Wendelle Stevens have collected some over the years. ET craft have a radar signature as reported by witnesses of the Disclosure Project and according to military and civilian aircraft witnesses. Billy Meier is a notable exception, wherein the Pleiadians posed to allow him to photograph their ships that appear to be made from metal. Pictures of ET craft, such as those from Billy Meier, can be verified as true because they were taken before the advent of digital photography and photo software. We have few photos of actual extraterrestrial beings; they have, of course, been portrayed in a number of ways in various science fiction movies.

From my perspective, it is most important to view most of our star brothers and sisters from a benevolent perspective. With one exception, I have seen nothing of which to be fearful. I have consistently put out a loving attitude and I have received it in return. This is in direct contrast to the portrayal of ETs in most books and movies—darkness and evil sell books and movies to a humanity mired in the fear of the 3rd Dimension.

DENIAL: The scientific community continues to dismiss the reality of extraterrestrials and UFOs. The official position of the government of the United States is to continue to deny everything about extraterrestrials and UFOs. There have been no admissions about joint projects with extraterrestrials or the reverse engineering of their technology — nor do I expect any in the future. Governments in other countries have released some information, but continue to deny any direct involvement with extraterrestrials.

For the most part, the major media in the U.S. ignores anything about UFOs or extraterrestrials. Outside the U.S., the media is much more open to the whole subject of UFO sightings and ETs.

REVERSE ENGINEERING: Based on testimony from a number of credible human sources, I believe that the technology from extraterrestrial craft has been reverse-engineered within projects under the U.S. Government, by other governments, and by U.S. Defense Contractors. These secret projects have resulted in technology advances from Velcro to integrated circuits to actual ET spacecraft. I wrote about this in the *Paradigm Trilogy*. I believe that many sightings of UFOs today are of reverse-engineered craft, flown by Earth humans. Niara Isley was on a base on the moon when she was in the U.S. military, demonstrating the degree to which the public has been denied the truth about extraterrestrials.

In Summary

I know that extraterrestrials are visiting Earth and are walking among us. I also know there are trillions of physical beings throughout the universe. With the exception of some who come from this sector of the universe, I believe that all of these off-planet beings are benevolent, with many living in higher states of consciousness. I believe that most are humanoid, but that they may or may not appear like our physical form.

I believe that UFOs are here to gradually awaken humanity to the fact that we are not alone in the universe and that there are technologies and events greater than those reported in the popular media, or admitted by governments. I believe that some ETs are here to help us awaken to our larger spiritual nature.

I believe that scientists have reverse-engineered ET technology. In an attempt to preserve positions of power, based on my own multiple experiences, I know that the whole subject of extra-terrestrials and UFOs is being covered up and distorted.

2

Beings with Physical Form

The physical universe, as observed through telescopes of Earth humans, is about 93 billion light years in diameter. The stars we see at night with our naked eyes are all within the Milky Way Galaxy. We also can see other galaxies such as Andromeda. The physical universe appears to be a three-dimensional sphere that stretches to infinity. Scientists estimate its age at 13.8 billion years. It appears to our eyes, telescopes and instruments to be mostly empty space. The distance to the nearest star, Proxima Centauri, is 4.2 light years. Is it any wonder that the scientific community discounts the presence of sentient life anywhere near Earth? It would take them many years to travel here. This was my point of reference in 1996 when I left the business world, and took a college level course in astronomy.

However, as recited in the foregoing chapter, I have seen evidence that extraterrestrials are here. And I believe they have been here for a long time. The following reports are compilations from various human sources. They are of the major off-planet races that have "visited" Earth over the years, interacting with the humans of this planet, both to our benefit and not. Keep in mind that these reports are from Earth humans describing something that is inherently strange to them, and that their emotions and backgrounds come through their words.

Pleiadians

The Pleiades are a cluster of stars located in the constellation Taurus. Pleiadians, also known as Nordic aliens, are humanoids and very similar in appearance to Earth humans; they come from several planetary systems of the Pleiades.

Pleiadians want to help Earth and help humanity ascend to higher dimensions; there are reports that some of this race, in the past, have not acted in the best interests of Earth humans.

Most Pleiadians are more highly evolved spiritually than the average Earth human. They reside at higher frequencies that are lighter than what 3rd Dimension humans know. They can switch between the 3rd and the 9th Dimensions, or anywhere between.

The Pleiadians believe that eventually all will become Pure Light at the center of creation, which is God/Spirit. As we evolve, gaining wisdom and true understanding about our real essence, we will begin to open up more to Love, and to feel our connection with one another and the universe.

Arcturians

They originate from a crystal blue planet orbiting the star Arcturus, a red super-giant located in the constellation Bootes. Arcturians are the most advanced civilization in this Galaxy, operating in the 5th Dimension and above. They exist mostly in a spiritual plane of thought and consciousness; they do not have a physical form, as we know it.

Arcturians appear to be 3 to 4 feet in height, with a greenish-blue skin and large oval eyes. They are quite telepathic. Their life span is believed to be 350-400 years. They do not eat like Earth humans, but live on positive forms of energy. They age slowly and do not fall prey to sickness. In Arcturian civilizations, professions and life's paths are chosen by one's spirituality level. The birth process is unlike ours; it consists of a female and male mentally bonding, from which a clone of the bond is produced.

Their mission is to assist our spiritual development. They are spiritual, mental, and emotional healers for Earth humans. They believe that love is the primary requirement. Arcturians serve as guardians of Earth, protecting us from civilizations that would interfere with our development.

Sirians

The brightest star visible from Earth is Sirius in the constellation Canis Major. Sirians have been directly involved with Earth in times past, and therefore take an interest in our current situation. As with all ETs, there are some members of their civilization who are in "service to self," while others are in "service to others." They appear human, but are much more technologically and spiritually evolved than Earth humans.

Sirians are a much older civilization. Their ancestors were part of the seeding of Earth's multi-race civilization. They were present on Earth in ancient Egypt.

They have come at this time to help us raise our vibration, and to help us remember our purpose for this lifetime. They believe we have evolved to the point of individual and planetary liberation. The Pleiadians and Andromedans are working with the Sirians. They see themselves as "Spiritual Warriors."

Lyrans/Vegans

According to several reports, the initiation of humanoid beings in physical form began in the constellation Lyra. This was long before any human race was on Earth. The Lyran races are of a Caucasian type.

Another foundational race is from Vega, in the Lyran constellation. The Vegan races are more representative of the darker skinned races on Earth: Native American, East Indian and aborigine. Vegans, along with Lyrans, seeded humanoid civilizations throughout the Milky Way Galaxy.

The Vegans were the first race here on Earth, during the time of prehistoric creatures. Earth then was considered a future Vegan colony, after the planet settled down. Since Vega is close to Earth in light years, this was very natural.

The Lyrans came to colonize and at some point Earth became a Lyran planet. Generations later, the Sirians came to claim Earth, and conflict ensued between the Sirians and the Lyrans.

The Sirians had knowledge of and cared about humanity

enough to occasionally give a little something so that primitive Earth humans would develop. The Lyrans acted like custodial gods who were more concerned with keeping Earth humans subverted. These dynamics, carried along in our genetic makeup, have been played out within Earth humans ever since.

Zetas

Zeta Reticuli is a binary star in the southern constellation of Reticulum. The Zetas are a race of tall grey aliens who became sterile during their long war with the Draconians, and who rely on cloning to replicate themselves. They saw Earth as a prime target to retrieve their lost abilities.

They worked with the Nazis in their efforts to create a master race. When this was not successful, they turned their attention to the United States with the importing of ex-Nazi scientists and masterminds after WWII. They were able to secure an agreement with the U.S government to exchange experiments with the DNA of human abductees for advanced technologies.

Working from underground bases, such as near Dulce, New Mexico, they have been behind abductions of humans and cattle mutilations in the American Southwest. Their cloned-out emotions made them unaware of the fear they were inducing in their human subjects. The technology received from the Zetas has been contained in secret programs by the Illuminati in their quest for control of the U.S. population.

Draconians

Draco is a constellation in the far northern sky. Draco is circumpolar for observers in the Northern Hemisphere. The reptilian entities from Alpha Draconis have been active on Earth for many years. They made their first recorded appearance in Sumerian tablets. Reportedly, they are able to assume human forms as the controllers of the Illuminati. They also worked with the Nazis.

Like the Zetas, after WWII they turned to the United States. Here they support the efforts of those humans who seek to dominate humanity, the Illuminati. They also support those who see military action as a solution to conflicts. With their advanced genetic technology, they were able to implant their genetic codes into many of the founding fathers of the United States. They sometimes work with the Zetas and at other times are in conflict with them.

Anunnaki

Another race that has influenced events and the peoples of Earth came from the planet Nibiru. This planet circles our Sun every 3,500 years, dispatching visitors to Earth when in close proximity.

It is purported that Earth humans worshipped the Anunnaki as gods and goddesses in ancient Sumeria, Babylonia, and Assyria. A recent predicted invasion was thwarted when the orbit of Nibiru was altered so that this infrequent visitor did not pass in close proximity to Earth during its most recent orbit.

Short Greys

Many reports of encounters with off-planet beings involve the short greys: entities about 3 feet tall with grey skin and large almond eyes. They are EBEs (extraterrestrial biological entities), or biologically engineered robots. The tall greys and reptilians use them for various tasks.

Andromedans

The Andromeda Galaxy is the nearest galaxy to ours and has about one trillion stars, more than twice the number in the Milky Way Galaxy. There are many types of Andromedans, just as there are many different beings in our Milky Way Galaxy. There are at least twenty-eight different races. The Andromedans who are

21

currently interacting with Earth humans are from the star system Zenetae.

Andromedans are a telepathic race. Female Andromedans are 7 to 8 feet tall and the males are 7 to 10 feet tall. Andromedans can weigh as much as 600 pounds. They are thousands of years ahead of us technologically and are a spiritually advanced race. They are descendants of Lyrans.

The Andromeda Galaxy was untouched by the fall of consciousness, thus the physical beings from that galaxy function at higher vibrations.

Andromedans have been involved with Earth and with humans at various stages of our development. They say they have been invited by the Guardian Archangels of Earth to participate in our development. Reports indicate that hundreds of thousands of Earth humans have an Andromedan origin soul — more than from any galaxy other than the Milky Way Galaxy.

The frequency of Andromeda is much different than that of our galaxy and appears to affect the ease of incarnation and the amount of soul energy that can be maintained in the human form. They have quiet demeanor that has a great potency to affect others with their presence.

Andromeda Council

Tolec is the current designated contact person on this planet for the Andromeda Council. According to him, his soul essence was originally birthed on the planet Dakote, one of four planets in the Taygeta star system, located in the open star cluster of the Pleiades. During this lifetime on Earth, Tolec has been in contact with various representatives of the Andromeda Council since 1963, when they first brought him to their primary, flagship biosphere. His contact and communication with them continues today.

The Andromeda Council is an inter-dimensional governance and development body of aligned benevolent star systems and planets of sentient life for worlds in both the Milky Way and Andromeda galaxies. As a high-level governance body the Council is responsible for setting precedence, protocols, conditions of behavior regarding planetary exploration and first contact, new membership, and trade relations among its member planets. Think of it as a deep space United Nations.

Its own conduct is guided by, measured and adhered to by the highest degree of intergalactic standards, ethics and protocols. Every decision it makes is very cautious and deliberate. The Council itself is held responsible to a very rigorous set of governing laws and mandates.

The "Galactic Federation" is the operational management company of the Andromeda Council. Their deep space forces are responsible for day-to-day management and enforcement of the cooperative protocols for: intergalactic, interstellar, and inter-planetary trade, barter, exchange of resources, products and services, societal, cultural, and educational exchange, and many other activities on a planet-to-planet basis.

The Galactic Federation is comprised of approximately 140 star systems, and at present has 300 planets in its membership. It has its own sitting council representing its own star systems and planets. This council is led by a Chairman from the Tau Ceti star system. The Galactic Federation is a senior member of the Andromeda Council.

The "Galactic Federation of Light" was formed and has its base of operations in the Sirius B star system. Its founders are Draco Reptilians. It was formed relatively recently, approximately 1,000 years ago, though they claim differently. It is important to note the difference between the two organizations.

Not long ago, the Andromeda Council made a collective decision to override the Prime Directive of non-interference because they determined that the humans of Earth did not have the knowledge or tools to defeat the aliens in their midst. The Andromeda Council determined that humanity deserved a chance to evolve on its own without outside interference.

The subsequent war in space between forces under the auspices of the Andromeda Council and the Reptilians and Greys is now finished, with the Andromedan allies triumphant. The primary reason for this war was to eliminate the effects of thousands of years of negative energies beamed to Earth as well as negating etheric implant technologies used to keep humanity in a state of fear.

All underground and deep undersea bases of the Reptilians and Greys on Earth have been dismantled or destroyed by the Kaena people of the Procyon star system, a senior member of the Andromeda Council. Isolated earthquakes of an unusual nature and in unusual places are reportedly the results of the destruction of these Draco and Hydra Reptilians' underground bases.

ABDUCTIONS: I have had conversations with people who have had interactions with a variety of off-planet beings whom they describe as both frightening and benevolent. Some of them say that this began when they were small children and continues to present time. Having overcome their initial fright, those in this group look forward to further interactions with extraterrestrials. I know one individual who, despite his intense fear, continues to encourage contact with the short greys.

In stark contrast to these are those individuals whose experiences were totally frightening, who show the marks of physical abuse, and who do not want more encounters. I do not discount reports such as these as there are too many to be the products of human imaginations. I do believe, in individual cases, that emotional reactions to such events could, depending on the consciousness of the individual involved, produce reports of violence.

Then there are the cases where humans, dressed like aliens, are involved in abductions. Again there are too many of these to dismiss them. Here, I believe that those Earth humans who behave in this manner wish to instill fear in their fellow Earth humans for purposes of control; they prey on susceptible people.

DARK ALIENS: Reports about dark aliens and their recent history with humanity abound. (I call them "reports," not to diminish them, but because I have had no personal experiences with them.) These reports originated in channeled messages from a number of off-planet sources, and continue to be referenced in current communications. These reports were sensationalized in Internet postings almost from their inception. I find it interesting that people seem to be much more interested in discussing these dark aliens than talking about benevolent interactions with ETs.

In my early writing I portrayed dark aliens in a conspiracy with a group of humans who sought to control humanity. These characterizations are woven into the story line of the *Paradigm Trilogy*. I portrayed both off-planet entities and this group of humans as self-centered, without feelings for the majority of the people of Earth, and as an alliance between the disingenuous who seeks to take self-advantage at every opportunity. I still believe that this situation has been the case for many, many years — dating back to prehistoric times. Other writers have similarly portrayed this and continue to do so. However, the main theme of my books is about benevolent ETs who visit Earth and contribute to our positive evolution.

From my current perspective, none of the Zetas, Draconians, or Anunnaki were responsible for the fear-based 3rd Dimension civilization of Earth. They came here well after the fall of consciousness. At the time they made their appearance on Earth, they found a primitive people and saw that they could take advantage of them with their superior technology and knowledge.

PHYSICAL EVIDENCE: The Internet has carried reports of skeletons as tall as 18 feet. They have been unearthed everywhere from Alaska to Texas to Wisconsin in the United States, from India to Turkey to South America. Some archeologists attribute them to the Anunnaki. Similarly giant heads have also been excavated in many sites around the globe. Reports of things such as this have not reached the mainstream media, and/or have been presented in such a way that viewers dismissed or quickly forgot them.

There is no physical evidence of UFOs or extraterrestrials in the hands of the public or on display. I believe that such evidence does exist in the hands of certain operations within governments and corporations. The complete cleanup from incidents such as Roswell is testimony to the intense scrutiny and secrecy that the whole subject of off-planet beings is held by the intelligence community and others who know about such things.

MOON RISING: On February 25, 1994, 1.8 million photos were taken of the moon during NASA's Clementine Mission. This mapping of the surface of the moon is posted on the USGS site. The groundbreaking video "Moon Rising" is based on these photos; in it we see Earth's moon in vivid color. We also see saucer-shaped craft hovering over the surface of the moon and structures on the surface of the moon. Since viewing this video, I have not been able to look at the moon the same.

MASS LANDING: Much in the literature about extra-terrestrials and UFOs revolves about the prospects for a mass landing of starships and peoples from distant planets, all intended to rescue us from our current paradigm. I believe that such an event would throw the majority of the world's population into abject fear — not at all what those hoping for it intend. This heavy-handed way to overwhelm evil has been depicted in movies and books as the occasion for a military response against the invaders, rather than the peaceful outreach sought by those who want to be rescued.

In Summary

I believe that "visitors" from star systems such as from the Pleiades, Sirius, Reticuli, Alpha Draconis, and Arcturians, from the planet Nibiru, from the Andromeda Galaxy, plus others have interacted with Earth humans over many thousands of years and in numerous ways. (According to one reliable source, the U.S. military has identified 57 different off-planet races.) On planet Earth they discovered a beautiful, diverse ecology with many life forms unlike those of their home planets.

Evidence of their presence can be found in pyramids (on almost every continent), and among the buildings, hieroglyphs, petroglyphs, and traditions of ancient peoples. The Nazca Lines, a series of ancient geoglyphs located in the Nazca Desert of Peru, is further evidence of ancient off-planet presence. In recent times, there are the reported sightings such as in the prior chapter and crop circles in England that defy any reasonable explanation other than extraterrestrial involvement.

I believe that now there are very few dark aliens currently on this planet, and that the energy behind the cabal or secret government is the result of leftover momentum. I believe that remnants of their earlier organizations are still in existence, but that these are weakening daily. Much of the dysfunctional government of the United States, the widening gap between rich and poor, unrest in monetary systems, and continuing international violence is due to those who seek to retain wealth and power despite the loss of energy from their off-planet overseers.

I do NOT believe that extraterrestrials will come to save us. My current understanding is that highly conscious Earth humans are being shown the way to return Earth to its preeminent status before the fall of consciousness, and that this is the reason that many of us are here.

In the many visits of extraterrestrials to Earth, I see not only an explanation for some of our physical manifestations, but perhaps more importantly genetic memories that form the basis for some of our fears and imagination. Primitive man undoubtedly acknowledged these vastly superior creatures, and in some cases worshipped them.

I offer gratitude and appreciation to my star brothers and sisters for showing me their perspectives, and for working with me as I wrote the *Paradigm Trilogy*, and for communicating with me so that I might post their messages; this has been an important step towards my current consciousness. I look forward to interacting with my star brothers and sisters in peaceful and loving ways — after we of Earth have lifted ourselves to the higher consciousness of 5th Dimension and beyond.

The One

From our position as one with Prime Creator, we will now comment on those that Mark calls extraterrestrials, residents of the many planets of the multitude of star systems within the physical form of this universe. We see unique individual expressions of Prime Creator pursuing lives in physical form. We see that they are incarnating on different planets in order to gain experiences, as are you. We see that they have lifetimes in what you would consider wondrous and beautiful surroundings of peace and harmony. We see that they have lifetimes in places that you would consider to be dark and without light. For in order to experience all for Prime Creator, all must be experienced; plus experiences in the dark confirm desire to be of the light. We see that each is loved and held in high esteem by Prime Creator. We too hold all in oneness, for all are our brothers and sisters.

Your perceptions of them are highly colored by what you have been taught by those who would control your thoughts. Do not fear or judge them, for they are you and you are they. And if perchance you meet another from a distant planet, greet him or her as a brother or sister with love and acceptance.

Do they have technologies that you do not have? Yes, some

possess advanced technologies, other do not. Are they more conscious than you? Some are, some are not. And just like your earthly brothers and sisters, some will love you and some may harm you. Just remember we are all children of Prime Creator.

The aspects of the 3rd Dimension delineated above are the remaining momentum of that old paradigm that had Earth humans in its grasp for so long. Now what remains is the momentum of that earlier way of being. The underpinnings of the 3rd Dimension were removed; still many cling to the old ways of separation, fear and polarity. It will take some time for all of humanity to ascend to a higher consciousness. In the meantime, recognize these aspects of the old ways for what they are and learn to walk among them as necessary for your physical body, but do not allow them to overwhelm you.

As you observe the interactions with non-human beings, as cited by Mark, you may not see them as we do. We see the results of these many years of outside influences from off-planet races resulting in a human race capable of evolving into beings of higher consciousness who will be a new standard for all in the universe. Without these many external influences, each providing their contribution, this would not have been possible. The humans of the new Earth will indeed be wondrous beings.

The universe of physical form is indeed vast. Distances are measured not in feet, meters, or miles, but in light years. There are millions of stars in your galaxy, and many, many more galaxies beyond. Within each galaxy there are millions of star systems and millions of planets. Your telescopes are just beginning to see and measure the extent of this universe.

Layer upon this vastness the fact that there are trillions of inhabited planets, each with diverse life forms. Yes, you have many, many brothers and sisters of physical form, many different races, and many levels of development. Furthermore, know that each of these myriad life forms is an individualized aspect of Prime Creator, as are you. Now appreciate how special is this planet that you call Earth. For much attention is being focused upon it as it regains its stature as a planet of light, love and unity. Contemplate these revelations to glean the truth about who you really are.

3

Archangels and Ultraterrestrials

This material is new, or very new to me. I had heard about Archangels since I was a growing up as a good Catholic boy, but had paid them little attention. Now, from my higher state of consciousness I have a much different perspective. Over the last four years I have heard channeled messages from them and have been led in experiences of the non-physical by them. Their guidance has transformed my life.

After I had written a few chapters of this book and was looking for confirmation of where it was headed, I was fortunate enough to have a session with Archangel Michael with Joan Walker acting as an intermediary. In it he gave me words of encouragement about what I was writing and offered to assist as I went about creating its words. It has been my great pleasure to have his assistance as I have written this book. I am most grateful and appreciative.

Prior to entering into conversations with Archangel Michael, I knew nothing about Ultraterrestrials; I had not even heard the word before. Now I am being told that it is important that we grasp just how huge the totality of creation is, and how important we are in the overall scheme of things. Thanks to my communications with the Archangels, I have learned that we are on the front line of transforming Earth and all in this universe to higher levels of consciousness.

Archangels

These great beings of Light have helped me understand that physical form is much different from the non-physical, and how the dense physical form we take for granted exists only in our sector of this universe. Other parts of our universe have a different type of physical form, as do other universes. The Archangels have allowed me to experience the vastness of the non-physical realms of our universe and how they are a thousand times larger than what we can see and measure as our physical reality.

The first important thing that the Archangels impressed upon me is that the non-physical creates the physical; our immense physical universe came from the creative actions of non-physical beings. Using their creative skills, and employing the elements of earth, air, water and fire, non-physical beings created physical form.

The second was that when I raise my energies sufficiently, I could be in unity consciousness with them. I have found this to be the case as my consciousness has gradually risen, as I have experienced the non-physical, and as I have come to appreciate more about who I am. I would like to tell more about my experiences in the non-physical but words fall short of telling it.

They have told me that darkness, due to the fall of consciousness, exists only in this sector of the Milky Way Galaxy, and that only here do we find beings with the barest minimum Light of Source, just enough to keep them alive. They have helped me realize just how special our planet, Earth, is and why she is the focal point of the universe. Lastly, and most important, they have shown me who we, Earth humans, are and why we are so important.

The following list of Archangels is a commonly available listing. It was complied from several sources, usually associated with Judeo-Christian religions. I have come to know some of them in other distinctive and enlightening ways through channeled information and in the experiences through which they have led me. I consider my relationship with them to be very special.

This list is based on names that Earth humans have given to them. On other planets, they would most likely have different names. The functions listed below are the ones commonly associated with them, but do not disclose who these great beings really are and how intimately they are able to interact with us. Also this list does not detail my experiences with them.

Archangel Ariel: The name means "Lion or lioness of God." She supports healers, teachers and service workers and environmental causes.

Archangel Azrael: The name means "Whom God helps." Azrael's role is primarily to cross people over to heaven at the time of physical death.

Archangel Chamuel: The name means "He who sees God." Chamuel helps you find a career best suited for your purpose and passion.

Archangel Gabriel: The name means "God is my strength." She is the messenger angel. She supports writers and journalists.

Archangel Haniel: The name means "Glory of God." She is a nurturing mother who is able to care for you and create miracles.

Archangel Jeremiel: The name means "Mercy of God." In addition to being an Archangel of prophetic visions, Jeremiel helps newly crossed-over souls to review their lives.

Archangel Jophiel: The name means "Beauty of God." Jophiel helps us to think beautiful thoughts and to therefore create, manifest, and attract more beauty into our lives.

Archangel Metatron: He helps with chakra clearing. He once walked the earth as a human. He was the prophet and scribe Enoch.

Archangel Michael: The name means "He who is like God." His chief function is to rid the earth and its inhabitants of the toxins associated with fear.

Archangel Raguel: The name means "Friend of God." He is concerned with divine order, clairsentience and relationship harmony.

Archangel Raphael: The name means "God heals." Raphael is

a powerful healer of physical bodies, both for humans and animals.

Archangel Raziel: The name means "Secret of God." He is the Archangel of clairvoyance, spiritual understanding, and reclaiming your power.

Archangel Sandalphon: The name means "Brother" in Greek, a reference to his twin brother, Archangel Metatron. The twins are the only Archangels in heaven who were mortal men. He can help you be kind and gentle, yet powerful.

Archangel Uriel: The name means "God's light." Uriel is the Archangel of claircognizance. He can enlighten our minds with divine inspiration.

Archangel Zadkiel: The name means "The righteousness of God." He is the Archangel of clairaudience, who can help us hold mercy and compassion towards others and ourselves.

COMMENTS: During the last four years, I have had the great pleasure of interacting with Archangels Gabriel, Metatron, Michael, Raphael, Uriel and Zadkiel, and with Melchizedek, who I understand is also an Archangel. From them I have received insights into who I am, why I am here, the history of Earth, and where we all are headed. Moreover, I have received from them exquisite experiences in non-physical form and in non-form.

My understanding of three of these Archangels is that Michael is charged with directing the many energies of Source for this universe; Metatron is the overseer of this physical universe, and that Melchizedek keeps record of all activities in this universe. In addition, these three Archangels also act as Lords of Light overseeing the activities of the Creator Gods of this universe.

My interactions with the Archangels — initially through Mastering Alchemy, then via Joan Walker, and now directly with Michael — have produced a new me. I am most grateful for what I have been given, and for who I am. I look forward to future interactions.

Ultraterrestrials

Our physical universe is indeed vast with its billions of galaxies and trillions of planets. However, beyond physical form lies an even more immense arena of creation, the non-physical. This non-physical arena is home to a vast assemblage of beings of form. Then there are other universes — way beyond my scope of imagination. Archangel Michael has specified for me that all that lies beyond Earth and the extraterrestrials is to be known as the realm of the Ultraterrestrials, including the Archangels and Ascended Masters of this universe. These great beings of Light are a collective of the many aspects of Souce.

In the original creation of form, Source authorized many beings to occupy many universes. Each universe was to operate according to a different set of principles, plans and objectives. Each was to contain myriad life forms ranging from the barely visible to the totally visible. Each was to be constructed with places — not all were spheres — upon which or within which many beings could dwell. Thus creation is much more massive than one might expect upon observation from the perspective of one in physical form.

The universe of which we are a very small part was named "Thesus." It was to be the home of beings according to the life principles of love and unity. The beings of this universe were to fulfill the desire of Source to know Itself according to the design, principles and objectives laid out before creation. This was known as the "Universe Master Plan for Thesus." The plans for other universes were different, encompassing different designs, principles and objectives.

Oversouls were created in Thesus and charged with experiencing this blueprint. These great beings are both magnificent and powerful. Each is slightly different so that their adventures are unique. In order to encompass as much experience as possible, each was given the ability to express individual souls simultaneously for lifetimes in form. So each of these oversouls set out to experience themselves in multiple ways, and in turn experience all for Source.

Source desired to know as much as possible of the experiences of these great beings of light, so It created beings known as Archangels. They were charged with observing the great beings of light who were having experiences and reflecting these experiences back. A collective of Archangels is unique to each universe.

In the beginning there were only a few Archangels created to undertake this function. But as the great beings of light went about having their myriad experiences, there became a need to create more and more Archangels to continue to reflect all of the experiences that were occurring.

After a time had elapsed in Thesus (not linear time), Creator Gods were brought into existence by Source. They were to experiment with creating in ever more dense form. They went about this task creating initially a universe of barely physical form, much less than we imagine today. We might look upon it as gaseous. This was highly successful and beings of form enjoyed playing in this initial form. Then the Creator Gods began to experiment with ever more dense forms until a physical universe was created with its myriad stars and planets.

In the meantime, the other universes were taking form, each according to its particular set of principles, plans and objectives. Within each universe great beings of light were to experience according to each one's uniqueness. And once again there were Archangels created to reflect back to Source the great number of experiences that were under way. Source was most happy with Its many creations. For It was within each, and experienced Itself in every corner of Its many universes and Its many creatures of form.

Not long after the initial creations took place, the Archangels that were specific to Thesus were asked to take on the role of coordinating the activities of the Creator Gods within Thesus. Thus the functions of the Lords of Light became their responsibility.

The collective of Archangels, and other beings from the various universes that surround Source, along with the many, many other beings of form, comprise the realm of the Ultraterrestrials. This concept is provided for those of us in physical form to help us understand the vastness of creation.

The One

We communicate with you this day with a message about who we are as a grouping of Ultraterrestrials. Our perspective is somewhat different than that of the Archangels for we are not assigned solely in the universe of Thesus. We view all that happens within your universe, in non-physical form, in physical form, and in non-form, and we do it from the viewpoint of dispassionate observers who are associated with other universes as well.

We are most pleased to be able to communicate with you and to offer our insights. We highly value our relationships with the Archangels of this universe, and support their work, particularly with regards to the transformation of Earth. We request all humans of this planet to join with this historic ascension of consciousness, for your energies are needed.

Chrysalis

4

God, Form, and the Non-Physical

Before we venture further into realms beyond our everyday experiences, I propose we look at a number of concepts. If these appear old to you, you might be surprised to find herein new ways of looking at things.

I trust you are enjoying this book as much as I have enjoyed writing it. For me it has been a real eye-opener as I have dug back into what I had put aside in search of developing higher consciousness.

One purpose of this book is to tie together what I knew and what I believed from what had been my extraterrestrial point of view with what I now know, understand and believe from my experiences in the non-physical. From my recent experiences I now know that there are many, many non-physical beings in the universe, and that I have had intimate connections to some of them. From my more recent experiences I have a good understanding about who I really am — not in every detail, but certainly a good grasp of the major points — and I know how I fit within this larger picture. I invite you into my perspective, for I see that we all will eventually come to know each other as brothers and sisters and will discover the many facets of our larger reality.

I have assembled the following with assistance from Archangel Michael, and other Archangels and Ascended Masters. They will serve as a great reference source as we proceed to discuss who we all are, the transformation of humanity to higher states of consciousness, the emergence of the Christed planet Earth, and why we all are here.

Source

Growing up, I learned about God. Even in my darkest moments of fear and loneliness as a young man, I clung to knowing that there was a God. The Bible talked about God creating everything in seven days; it also talked about a God of wrath and judgment. I rejected all of that. Even when I rejected my Catholic upbringing and its portrayal of Jesus, I did not reject the notion that there was a God. But at best, my notion of God was fuzzy. The scientists, those who are always looking for a rational explanation for everything, came up with the "Big Bang" theory to explain the creation of the universe, and evolution to explain Earth and how we humans got here. That satisfied me for a while, until I began to question the complexity of our physical bodies and the extent of the universe. And I did not see how God fit into that theory.

My experience with people who adhere to one or another religion is that they are generally good people, in that they value family life, adhere to a more or less strict morality, and believe in life after death. That is not to say that all are alike, for there are some who manifest a religious exterior on Sundays while following less than upstanding lives on the other days of the week. Like people with no religious affiliation, all are trapped in aspects of the 3rd Dimension, accept the darker side of life through eyes of fear, separation, and judgment, and believe that this is the way things have always been and hope that all will someday be better. I now know that there is a higher consciousness than religion, and that this higher consciousness will lead us to a totally new way of being for all of humanity.

After my awakening in 1987, I was presented with the *Urantia Book*. In it I found a complex portrayal of the Trinity of God and descriptions of all manner of angelic beings and energy controllers who created and managed the physical universe. In it, for the first time, I came to believe that there really were sentient beings on planets other than Earth, but there was no hint of them anywhere near my home planet. As soon as I saw my first UFO and learned about past lives, I put the *Urantia Book* aside.

I do believe that the *Urantia Book* has value, but it is like many channeled books: dated and incomplete. From my involvement with it and other books, I have learned that studying words in a book is no substitute for actual experiences. Yes, you can find essential information in books, including this one; they will give you the basis for believing and expanding your horizons. However, go beyond to find personal experiences that will give you the basis for knowing.

For me Source is the initiator and upholder of all creation. Source created the great beings of light and charged them to experience. Creation reflects Source's desire to know Itself more fully. The spirit of Source is within me. I am a part of Source. Earth humans use many names to describe Source: God, Creator, Prime Creator, Godhead, All That Is, etc. In this book I will use "Source."

Soul

Even in my darkest days, when I had abandoned religion and was searching for a new path, I believed that I had a soul — a small essence within me — and that it would survive my death. Since those days in spiritual darkness, when only my career as a businessman and venture capitalist was important, I have made a one-eighty.

Twenty years later, I know that I have a soul because I interact with it regularly. I now understand that my oversoul is enormous, many faceted, very complex, and multi-dimensional, and that my physical body is very tiny by comparison. A small part of my oversoul is attached to my body for this lifetime. My oversoul has many expressions in non-physical form and in non-form. Under the direction of the Archangels, I have experienced some of these various expressions of my oversoul, and understand that they all work together to make a unified field of consciousness that identifies who I am.

I have been told that my oversoul is eternal, and that I have had many lifetimes. My soul is much more than a spark of Divinity within my physical body. I have been informed that

I have had over one million lives in non-physical form and in physical form. This is true for all Earth humans. All of us incarnated before Earth came to be. We have incarnated on other planets, and we have incarnated in non-physical form, for our souls are always growing and expanding. We will have the opportunity to incarnate while Earth is in 5th Dimension and beyond, or we may incarnate in other realms and energies. I believe that my oversoul chooses where to incarnate based on its desire to experience and grow, and that these experiences can be at various levels of consciousness in the physical as well as in the non-physical and can be in various locations within this universe. From the perspective of my oversoul, I now view my time in this physical body as but a moment in eternity and as a minute place in creation.

Light and Love

Light is the basic building block of the cosmos, both for the physical and for the non-physical. The Light emanating from Source is unlimited. There are many types, frequencies, and forms of Light; many are not known to those of us in physical form; many are used in the non-physical. Light is slowed to create physical form.

Love is powerful: it transforms Light into various forms. It too comes from Source and is unlimited. The Love that we as humans in physical form know is but a small fraction of all of the forms and types of Love present in creation. As we advance in our consciousness, we will discover other forms of Light and Love.

Angels, Archangels, Ultraterrestrials
and Lords of Light

Angels are everywhere in this physical universe and in the non-physical. There are many types with many different tasks. Each Earth human has angels associated with him or her. Archangels were created shortly after that moment when our over-souls were created. While originally intended to reflect all of creation back to Source, in more recent times they have taken on many tasks associated with creation, managing energies, the physical universe, and interacting with individual beings of form. The Lords of Light create energies to support all aspects of physical creation; they are the overseers of the Creator Gods who fashioned the universe of physical form.

Angels, Archangels, and Lords of Light exist in collectives; they can manifest individual beings in non-physical form as spokespersons. We assign names to these individual manifestations, according to our particular language and backgrounds.

Archangels, and great beings of light from other universes, along with many, many beings of form in all universes, are all part of the collective that is known as Ultraterrestrials. The One who is offering comments throughout this book is a special grouping of Ultraterrestrials.

Because the non-physical is at least a thousand times more immense than the physical, the numbers of Ultraterrestrials are beyond my comprehension. Relatively few Ultraterrestrials know about the existence of the physical form of this universe.

Extraterrestrials

Extraterrestrials are physical beings, not native to Earth. Their physical form may appear to be something quite different than what we experience here on Earth. Taking into consideration all the millions of galaxies, there are trillions of other inhabited planets with millions of physical beings on each. Beyond the realm of the extraterrestrials is the realm of the Ultraterrestrials. When compared to Earth's civilization, ET civilizations vary in levels of technology and spiritual attainment, from primitive to advanced. All extraterrestrials from this sector of the Milky Way Galaxy have been impacted by the fall of consciousness.

Physical Form

The universe that we see in the night sky and through telescopes comprises physical form. It is indeed vast, almost beyond the comprehension of human minds. Most people believe that physical form is all there is: Earth, the Solar System, the Sun, and beyond that the stars and galaxies. Oh sure, some say, "I know I have a soul and I believe in God, but this is where I live. This is what I can touch and measure. This is what astronomers are telling me." Then they go on to point to themselves and everything around them and say, "All this stuff around me is what I mean by physical; I'm physical."

I have come to understand that physical form, my body, the Earth, and the stars and galaxies are all energy constructs: energy slowed into matter. Physical form energy constructs are brought into existence by the actions of the Creator Gods and the Elementals. Earth, air, water, and fire comprise the four elements of physical form. Additionally, as we shall see in a moment, physical form and 3rd Dimension are quite different. Some manifestations of physical form, such as quasi-physical or semi-physical, exist at higher dimensions. After all, I have seen an ET craft materialize out of the side of a mountain. Additionally, I saw more than one ET craft semi-materialize not far from our CSETI group displaying a beautiful array of scintillated blue light, and barely visible beings in semi-physical form around the CSETI groups.

Non-Physical Form

I separate physical form from non-physical form because of my experiences in non-physical form. I communicate telepathically with celestials, as well as physical beings from other planets. I have experienced the non-physical parts of my soul. This book is co-authored with Archangels. I am able to have conversations with an Archangel. All of these are examples of beings in non-physical form. Non-physical form involves energetic constructs, different from those used to create physical form, but nonetheless constructs of energy. Of course, the energies of non-physical form are much different than the physical. Individual non-physical beings are manifested from the collectives of non-form. The totality of non-physical form is many times more immense than is physical form.

Non-Form

I have come to know non-form, the greatest reality of all, vaster than non-physical form. Source is non-form. Form springs from non-form. Physical form, such as that of Earth, comes from non-physical form that was created out of non-form. I find these definitions extremely important as I go about exploring the larger reality. I now have had experiences in both non-physical form and in non-form, as well as my physical body. These experiences are amazing, wonderful, beautiful, and quite real.

If I could, I would eagerly reside in the non-physical, better yet I would reside in non-form. My experiences in the non-physical are like immersion in a warm swimming pool: surrounded by warmth, but still separate from my surroundings. My experiences in non-form are like allowing myself to merge with the water, like becoming one with no boundaries, a place where I feel perfectly at home. In non-form I feel totally at ease, totally loved, and embraced in warmth that is very familiar. After I experienced non-physical form and non-form, I quickly came to understand that everything is an energy construct. My body, as well as my environment, is an energy construct dictated by non-physical form that in turn is created by non-form.

3rd Dimension

The 3rd Dimension (AKA the conventional paradigm) is an energy construct of stability, rigidness and separation. Fear, judgment and violence derive from these basics. It is easy to get 3rd Dimension confused with physical form, but they are different. Our bodies are physical form; how we function in our bodies determines whether we are in 3rd Dimension or a higher vibration. How we relate to our surroundings, whether we see things as fearful and separate (3rd Dimension), or we see ourselves in oneness with everything (higher dimensions) determines our behavior. When we are surrounded by rigidness and separation, and operate based on fear, we really cannot make choices; we can only react. Many people on Earth are functioning as if they were still part of the 3rd Dimension; for many years I, too, functioned from the 3rd Dimension, but no longer.

4th Dimension

In 4th Dimension we remove ourselves from the separation, polarity and fear of 3rd Dimension. We are still in our familiar physical form and we still see our surroundings as physical. We can still get angry, but it is a different anger, not based on primal fear. We can still judge others and see separation. But we do not walk around fearing everybody and everything, and because we are not immersed in that feeling, we can make real choices, not just react as we did in the 3rd Dimension. Now we can begin to see the larger picture, and we can begin to discover who we really are. We remain in 4th Dimension until we can function at the higher energy level of 5th Dimension. Most people on this planet are now functioning from a 4th Dimension energy construct.

5th Dimension

Beyond 4th Dimension is a whole new ballgame, and it is the gateway to the higher dimensions. In 5th Dimension, physical form takes on a new meaning: physical form can be fluid rather than rigid. In 5th Dimension I discovered that I was part of a vast collective of beings ranging all the way to Prime Creator. I discovered my many past lives, found out that they are really concurrent lives, and found out that I will have many, many more. I discovered that I am an individualized essence of Prime Creator in a physical body. I discovered that I have unlimited choices as a co-creator. To remain in 5th Dimension, I am learning to control my every thought, every emotion, every word, and every action in every moment.

Christed Matrix

The Christed Energy is an aspect of Source. It is most easily characterized as unconditional Love, the Light of Source, and perfect Unity with all. The Christed Energy should not be confused with the term Christ as used by some religions to designate an individual or to refer to a lesser energy, for the Christed Energy or Christed Matrix is far beyond those limited perspectives.

I have within me a small Christed Matrix, as does every other human of this planet. There is a very large Christed Matrix at the center of Earth. These were installed on November 11, 2011. Each of us has the opportunity to activate the Christed Matrix within us, and by doing so open the way to our multi-dimensional self. In this book, references to a Christed planet mean that when the Christed Matrix within Earth and in each of us is fully activated, this planet will become a multi-dimensional sphere of Light, Love and Unity. And because we will then have done something that has never been done before, Earth will be a model for all in the universe.

Unity, Oneness, and Consciousness

These words have many definitions. Based on my experiences, I will use them as follows. Everything in the universe is conscious: Humans have an individual consciousness of how they see themselves and their surroundings ranging from 3rd Dimension to 5th Dimension and above. Animals have a group conscious sometimes mistaken for instinct. Plants have a consciousness, as do inanimate objects such as rocks. Almost all in the non-physical, those with form and that without form, possess consciousness of a much higher dimension than do I. (The lone exception to this is the astral plane, where souls with minimal light can reside.) Oneness and/or unity means recognizing that I am perfectly connected to all, and I give thanks to individual beings for providing me with their uniqueness.

Elementals

The Elementals are non-physical beings who use the four elements of earth, air, water and fire to create physical form, including the physical form of Earth humans. Using a fifth element, love, they were very involved in creating the architectural constructs of the original Earth of the 12th Dimension. They were also creators of the rigid 3rd Dimension, as well as the human body of the 3rd Dimension. They are now engaged in fashioning energetic constructs from a basis of love as a gradually transforming Earth returns to the 12th Dimension.

Time

Linear time is a construct that was installed as a part of 3rd Dimension, to assist Earth humans in coping with the vagaries of rigid physical form. There are several different types of time. In higher consciousness, time is simultaneous. Beings at higher levels of consciousness have difficulty translating what they perceive into linear time that can be shared with humans in lower frequencies. We shall encounter this particularly when we look at the history of Earth. This distinction is what makes forecasting of future events so difficult for non-Earth humans. In the larger picture of the non-physical, all is taking place in simultaneous time. All of what we might perceive as past lives are really taking place at this moment. Beyond the physical there is no past or future.

If you can imagine approaching an unfamiliar planet in a starship, you may appreciate the difficulties that extraterrestrials have in understanding our history according to an historical timeline, and in giving us any estimate of the time in which past events may have occurred or future events may occur. For Ultraterrestrials the task is even more difficult in that many have never been in physical bodies and have no points of reference in linear time. All of this makes pinning down dates, past or future, to convey to us almost impossible.

With the closing of 3rd Dimension and the movement to higher dimensions, linear time began collapsing on Earth. I am feeling time collapsing, as I compare events week to week, or think back to long ago events.

Collectives

Based on my experiences and observations, both the non-physical and non-form are collectives or a series of collectives. In this sense, a collective is a grouping of beings in that their energies are melded together into one. In non-form there are collectives of collectives and so on to infinity. Beings in form exist as part of a collective, manifesting one of their number as a spokesperson for the "we" of their collective. Some extraterrestrials function as part of a collective, remaining attached to the others of the collective in what they call a "hive mentality." As a human of Earth, I have a soul that has been individuated for this lifetime; however, the larger non-physical me is one with a collective that I call my spirit.

Channeling

Telepathic communications from extraterrestrials and non-physical beings to Earth humans can take several forms and have varied results. The factors that affect the quality and focus of channeled communications are as follows: The intent of both the transmitter and the receiver of the communication. Is it to be a general broadcast, to focus on a group, or to be specific to one individual? The clarity with which the communication is received depends on the vibration of the receiver: The higher the vibration, the clearer the communication.

I know from my own experience that when the receiver of a communication is fearful for any reason, then the message will have a fearful tone woven into it. I also know when a receiver is functioning from a higher/lighter vibration, then the message will have only a love-based tone. I have seen this in my own channeling and in the channeling of others. As I have progressed to functioning at a higher vibration, the clarity of my channeling has improved, as well as my access to beings of a higher dimension.

Beyond channeling there are on-going communications. Whereas channeling is more or less a one-way process — the receipt of a message that is intended to be spoken or written — on-going communication is an interactive mode between two more or less equal beings who are simply having a conversation. This conversation may involve new disclosures, may involve questions and answers, and may involve personal information for the beings involved.

In my particular situation, I currently interact with Archangel Michael as I compose this book. I can feel his presence as I type these words and receive suggestions. I also can have conversations with Adrial and my other Andromedan friends. This is in contrast to The One, where the communication while specific to this book, is very much a one-way transmission.

Knowing

I have been told that I have had many past lives, done many things, and incarnated in many different realms, other planets and in the non-physical. From these many prior lifetimes, I have a vast reservoir of wisdom based on lessons learned. I am able to draw upon that reservoir as I live my current life on Earth. This comes to me as knowingness. I am learning to rely on it as I write the words of this book and as I go about my daily life.

In Summary

I have come to understand the above concepts through experiences and knowingness, and through information gained by interacting with Ultraterrestrials. I have discovered more about who I really am through experiencing my greater non-physical self.

The One

The non-form is a vast arena of consciousness, many times more vast than is the arena of form, which is many times vaster than the arena of physical form. We Ultraterrestrials are a vast collective of powerful beings; we are of the original creation of the Godhead and have been here for eternity and will continue so in what you call the future. Our collective power is unlimited. Our love of all is unbounded. We are one with all. It is from our collective that the light of the Creator emanates to all in creation.

It is fair to say that we are of the highest dimensions. However, we are also multi-dimensional in that we can come to you and assist by producing these words, and we can give insight to you about anything you wish to know within your capability to comprehend. Do not be belittled by our presence, for we are one with you.

Do not depend upon the written word to understand all there is. Seek out experiences to enable your consciousness to rise to the heights. For it is through experiences that you will unveil yourself, as a multi-dimensional being of light and then you will know who you really are.

The messages we send to Mark are of a high order in that his vibration is high. We do not send messages if we detect that he is somehow fearful or otherwise disturbed or distracted. Thus it is with all who receive communications from the non-physical.

Chrysalis

5

Messages: Andromedans

I am very grateful to my brothers and sisters from Andromeda and the celestials associated with them aboard the starship, "Athabantian," for they started me on a path of raising my consciousness without which I would not be who I am today. Beginning with my writing of *Trillion*, and then more openly later, these great beings gave me the experience of transcribing their observations of humanity. Unknown to me until later, for my receiving skills and my consciousness were just developing in 1997, they were the ones who had silently coached me as I wrote the first book of the *Paradigm Trilogy*.

Then in 2008, as I stood in the kitchen of my home in Fort Collins, Colorado, they began more direct communications. "We want to give you information, and have you post it on your web site," they communicated telepathically. I replied, "No way, do you think I'm crazy?" After a repeat of this conversation several times, a month later I posted my first communication from Justine at "Mark's Corner." So named because I hoped no one would find it. Needless to say, many of you, my brothers and sisters of Earth, did find my postings, and translated them into many other languages. Thank you. I am very grateful for your support over the last seven years.

Later, I learned that Justine and Moraine, from whom I also received messages, had been friends of mine on Akima, a higher dimension imension planet in the Andromeda Galaxy. They were with me when I decided to incarnate on Earth at this wondrous time of the planet's transformation. After they had reincarnated in Andromeda, they volunteered to come aboard the starship "Athabantian" that was headed to Earth. "We found you," they communicated from high above Earth.

Bren-Ton, who is also from Andromeda, and who has evolved to a lighter vibration with a less physical body, came into the picture next and a different perspective was transmitted. After I moved to Pagosa Springs, Colorado, Ro-Tan began to channel through me to small groups. (It was really something the first time he showed up!) Later, Adrial (a "celestial" attached to Andromedans and currently aboard "Athabantian") came into my life with more observations about humanity and our planet. These communications from my off-planet friends can be found at: www.cosmicparadigm.com/marks-corner. My book, *Transformation*, is an organized collection of communications from my off-planet friends.

In early 2011, I was informed that my rational mind was interfering with communications at Mark's Corner (a reference to my focusing too much on negative Earthly events beyond my control). To clear the channel, all future messages were to be posted at: www.cosmicparadigm.com/Athabantian/. And I was no longer to provide my analysis and comments along with their messages. What followed was a series of communications, some from Taugth (another celestial working with the Andromedans); these led to the establishment of the Institute of Light and to the revelations about Abiquor (a higher dimension training facility in this area of Colorado). The urgings of Taugth and Adrial led to the Transformation 2012 workshop in August of that year — a very successful event, according to the 150 people involved.

As I reviewed my several hundred channeled messages to present excerpts here, several things struck me. *First*, the messages were clear, direct and insightful. Upon reading them again, I was surprised at the depth of the information that had been conveyed.

Second, my messages were definitely influenced by my mindset at the time I received them. I was particularly struck by my intense focus in 2008 to 2010 on the activities of the agents of the dark energy as I detailed their influence on all facets of our civilization. I now realize that I had been giving up my energy to some off-planet dark energy puppet master. I now see from a completely different perspective. As you will see in the remainder of this book, I no longer focus any attention in the direction of dark energy, or, for that matter, on most of the happenings in the conventional paradigm.

Third, a lack of light exists in some off-planet beings (humanoid and other), creating extraterrestrials who act from fear, separation, dominance and judgment. A lack of light in Earth humans results in similar behavior. All are very susceptible to the opinions of others and often fall into various addictions. Many of them fool themselves into believing that they are doing the right thing, either in opposing society, or becoming a domineering force in it. For example, replacing one 3rd Dimension dictatorship with another 3rd Dimension dictatorship solves nothing, as no fundamental change has occurred. I now see that overwhelming the dark by sending loving Light is the only way to change the dark. However, we cannot stop there; to completely overcome the dark, we must become the Light ourselves.

Fourth, I was highly influenced by the idea that something of great magnitude would transpire on December 21, 2012, something that everyone on the planet would recognize as the beginning of the New World. My postings reflected this. What had been expected did not happen, at least not in the way that many had anticipated. As I shall explain later, something of great proportions did happen in December of 2012, something almost beyond my comprehension.

Fifth, I did not understand the extent of Earth's transformation, and my own personal transformation to a being of Light. I was focused on extrapolating what I knew. The reality of what is now occurring is so much grander. I had not come close to realizing what the New Earth would be: A Christed planet of the 5th Dimension. (I will go into my understanding of this in subsequent pages.)

Below are excerpts from the communications I received from my Andromedan brothers and sisters, the celestials associated with them aboard "Athabantian," plus two special channelings.

The rest of the universe is closely watching the progress of these changes. For what transpires on Earth affects all. For what transpires on Earth sets a pattern for the ascension of all in physical form. Is it any wonder that so many of your star brothers and sisters are gathered on and about your planet, watching and assisting with these events?

— Bren-Ton   2-28-12

I am commenting from a starship of the Andromedans on what I observe happening on the surface of your planet. Please know that what is happening these days impacts all within this universe. Everything is interconnected, more than you would ever imagine. A saying of your planet, that the flapping of the wing of a butterfly in the Amazon is felt throughout your world, is quite true. Energetically, we are all connected.

— Justine   9-30-08

Each person has a unique path to pursue in this lifetime. Listen to your inner guidance to discern that path. Each of your choices can be aided by looking into your heart. As you read these words, you know that the heart energy is guiding you to a higher way to live, to a life free from attachments, to a way other than the conventional.

You volunteered to come to this planet as an example of the light. Become so in your own unique way. As you go about your daily routine, you can shine your unique light for all to see. Become a beacon. When many beacons of light shine forth, all will ascend to lighter densities.

— Moraine   12-9-08

There is great value in this 3rd dimensional experience. It should not be denied. Why else would your soul undertake such a difficult experience? All experiences in this 3rd dimension are desirable, those you may decide are good, and those you may decide are not so good. They all contribute to the growth of your soul; they are all experiences that your soul craves.

Do not diminish these experiences by choosing to ignore some aspect of them. That which surrounds you, the people, the setting, the climate, all are important to gain the fullness of the experience.

— Bren-Ton   11-17-08

What you as an individual should aspire to is to vibrate at a density in which you can relate to those with whom you desire a relationship. This does not mean that you need relate to everyone. By focusing your energy at a specific level, you will attract others whose frequency vibrates with yours. Determine what frequency feels most comfortable to you. Try out different frequencies to learn where you wish to reside in the moment.

— Adrial   7-3-09

The most important thing you can do in this lifetime is to tend to your own light, setting an example for those who observe you. You cannot change one of your sisters who is of the dark until your sister is ready to change. You cannot awaken one of your brothers who chooses to sleep until that brother wishes to awaken. Live in the light, giving an example of the highest way to conduct yourself.

— Adrial   8-10-09

The energy of Earth affects everyone on this planet. It is her call to pay attention to growing things, to animals, small and large, to think about the composition of the dirt in which you are planting. The energy of Earth is love for you, her humans. It is a beckoning to enjoy all of her majesty, whether on the high mountains, or beneath her seas. The energy of Earth calls to each of you to touch her, to smell, to listen to her silence, and to enjoy the magic of her animals, fish, and birds.

— Adrial   6-3-09

Oil companies are the epitome of large multi-national corporations. ... The demand for oil products has risen exponentially over the past hundred years, primarily due to its use in transportation. ...

The civilization of this planet is defined by oil more than by any other structure or material substance. There would be no widespread transportation of products around the globe without it, no grapes in the winter, no exotic foods from far off lands. Oil defines your modern civilization. Its burning is also one of the major things that has fouled your atmosphere, water and land. It also causes great harm to Earth, as it is extracted. ...

When we of the more advanced civilizations gave your inventors the recipes for the products of petroleum, they were intended as a transition to a higher level of evolution, not for the plethora of uses that have been developed in direct contradiction to the health of the planet.

— Bren-Ton   1-20-09

Once you see yourselves as basically good, you will begin to see that you are one with Earth who is basically good. Once you see yourselves as flawless, you will accept all your brothers and sisters on your planet as loving relatives, not as lesser beings. Once you see yourselves as flawless, you will see those of us from other planets as also flawless, and not immediately jump to the conclusion that we are evil.

— Bren-Ton   1-30-09

I offer the following to you as one who has observed your planet since its inception. Many of your enlightened brothers and sister of Earth have fallen into the trap of believing that some magical moment will happen wherein they will ascend to some higher dimension in an instant of time. Keep in mind that Earth is returning to her former self; this does not square with a perception of a magical ascension to take people off the planet.

— Adrial   9-4-09

Just because you do not have specific training to move to the higher frequencies does not mean that you will be unable to do so. Everyone who desires to accompany Earth to the higher way of being will come along. There will be difficulties along the way as your body and your environment change. You will have trouble assimilating to new ways of being, but no one who truly desires to ascend with Earth will be left behind. So set your intention to achieve this wondrous new way of being and come to our level of functioning. It is quite beautiful and loving here. We will welcome you each and everyone.

— Bren-Ton   6-25-10

On my travels I found people of different races, black, brown, and white, plus many different languages and different family habits. I saw everyone as my brother or sister. Everyone was human just like me, some small differences, but basically just other humans whether they were of high station or low. We were all just humans of this planet.

My enlightenment increased dramatically when I discovered knowingness that there were other inhabited planets. I was given the knowledge that my soul had incarnated on many of these. This too helped me see other Earth humans as my brothers and sisters, and allowed me to love them. This enlightenment and love for my fellow humans stemmed from the Christ energy within me, an energy that was apparent to all with whom I came into contact. ...

My primary purpose in incarnating on this planet was to bring the Christ energy to you and your ancestors. I did not intend to establish a religion. I did not come here to die for your sins. I came here to distribute the Christ energy, period.

— Jesus   2-2-09 & 2-14-09

I am a spokesperson for those aboard the starship "Athabantian." We are pleased to visit with you this morning. As we have previously communicated, when you are able to hold a 5th Dimension vibration you are indeed one with the collective of which are we. Thus we can communicate as friends, not as one somehow better than the other.

We intend the following message as encouragement for those who are willing to take the next step in their personal transformation. Read it in joy, for you have a grand adventure awaiting you.

Many have come from all parts of the Cosmos to participate in the great transformation of Earth. Mark, it was your choice to come here from Andromeda, to incarnate as a human, and to spend many years living as an ordinary human among your family, with your career, your friends and many others. This earlier activity was necessary for you to firmly connect with this planet and her people, to appreciate what life is like on a 3rd

Dimension planet.

For those reading these words, we come today to give you a better understanding of your current situation. We come as ones who knew you from your time on other planets, as ones who are neither better than nor less than the real you. All within the higher vibrations are equal; all respect each other within the oneness of the All That Is.

Never before has a planet mired in the 3rd Dimension raised itself to 5th Dimension functioning. The physical bodies of Earth humans are to be infused with the vibrations of the 5th Dimension. In the process all will be transformed into lightness. It is a grand undertaking, involving the most powerful of celestials; we are most happy to be a part of it. Moreover, we are extremely happy for all Earth humans who are actively participating in this grand undertaking.

Know that the celestial collective is a vast realm, much greater in numbers than you in physical form. In the celestial realm we are a pure collective. We know this is hard to grasp, but we are most comfortable in this way, for indeed once one moves above the frequency of physical form, all operate in a collective. There are many collectives, the celestials are but one of those who are without physical form. Then there are those with no form at all; this is an even vaster arena, and one that is impossible to convey in words. What is important to understand is that the non-form creates what is in form; what is in non-physical form creates that which is in physical form.

As a creature in physical form, you have a readily recognized individuality. It is easy to see and feel the limits of yourself. You can touch the limits of your body. You can feel your mental and emotional bodies. You can get in touch with your soul. Thus you are an easily defined individual. Within the celestial realm we are not so easily delineated. As we said before, we are a collective, and as such our form melds within the entire collective. When we wish to manifest an individual being such as I am doing at this moment, we do so from the collective.

We are belaboring this point because as you move into the higher vibrations, you too will lose aspects of your individuality. (The concept of the "rugged" individual exists only in the 3rd Dimension.) As one learns to exist in the 5th Dimension, you will begin to feel the closeness of others in the 5th Dimension. You will "know" that oneness is a feeling, a knowing-ness; it cannot be put into words.

We would like to remind all who read these words of the reason you incarnated on Earth. After you have the ability to sample the higher vibrations and can learn to maintain yourself in them, then you can now truly appreciate your reason for incarnating. It is quite simple: You possess a physical body. Now you must become adept at moving into the 5th Dimension. There you will assist other to do the same.

By focusing on this single objective, you will become an ascended one. Your light will shine for all with whom you come into contact. Your energy will radiate to all around you. By doing so you will have a significant impact on this planet and indeed all others in physical form throughout the cosmos. Those of us who have no physical form are unable to accomplish this. There are many Earth humans who do not have the ability (as yet) to be in the higher vibrations while in physical form. This is why each of you volunteered to come to Earth.

There are now enough lightworkers on Earth maintaining higher vibrations so that Earth's transformation is assured. As we have spoken of before, the magnetic constructs of the 3rd Dimension were removed in December 2012. This makes the way to the higher dimensions much easier, but by no means automatic. Individual physical forms must still take actions to train themselves to exist in these higher vibrations; it is not automatic. It is a daily discipline. To maintain yourself in the 5th Dimension, you must learn to control your thoughts and emotions. You have experienced yourself drop from a lighter vibration when a lower vibrations confronts you. You have also seen yourself maintain the lighter vibration when lower vibrations ask for your attention. You know the difference in your reactions. Practice this valuable lesson.

Look in the mirror and ask yourself, "What is important in my life? What am I doing that I would like to continue doing, doing more of? What can I do without? To what am I attached? What serves me? What serves the continuation of the 3rd Dimension?" Then decide how you will live.

Understand that you do not need external verification. The best use of your time and energy is to discover for yourself exactly who you are, why you agreed to incarnate at this time and place, and what you can do to further this. Forget about interacting with your space brothers and sisters. You already know in your heart that others of physical form exist on other planets. Do not waste your time seeking to see their ships, or listening to the witness of others; knowing that they are your brothers and sister is enough. As we have told you, they walk among you.

You do not need some higher authority such as your government or your religion to tell you that non-Earth human life forms exist. That is giving away your power (once again) to an authority that you have placed in charge of your life. Forget about ET sightings. Do you really need to see an ET ship in the sky time after time to realize that others exist in the universe? Look within yourself. Know that many from other planets walk among you. Know that many from other planets have incarnated to be with you at this time.

Be all you can be. Seek to raise your own energy. Practice daily. Focus your attention on this singular task. Compose yourself; do not flit from one message to another. Practice self-discipline. Practice discernment. Discover your energy field. Then see all that is not a part of you as merely entertainment on the stage of your life drama. Focus on being "The" player on your stage. Nothing else matters for your advancement. Nothing will happen by wishing for it to be true. You must do this for yourself; no one else can do it for you. Know that you are the creator of everything in your life experience; create well.

To remain within the higher vibrations, you must put aside all that draws you back into the 3rd Dimension. Put aside anger, judgment, wealth, and power over others. Put aside attachments to the material comforts of the 3rd Dimension. Be in the world, but not of it. Realize who you really are: An individuated expression of Source, a great being of light. Put aside past behaviors and current habits that do not contribute to the manifestation of your higher self in your body. Do not allow yourself to be pulled into the 3rd Dimension while wavering in your commitment to be in the 5th Dimension. Practice self-discipline, but do not forget to live in the joy of creation.

Know that the 3rd Dimension is going away. Know that your planet, along with all others in 3rd Dimension density, is being cleansed of the darkness. The glue of the 3rd Dimension has been removed. The energy construct that held all in 3rd Dimension rigidness is no more. The sense of freedom you may be feeling is due to this collapse, due to your lack of focus in the old ways.

You have an opportunity to be one of the first to be a great physical being of light, a powerful human to show the way to others. To do this, self-discipline is required. Self discipline to shed the judgment, violence, anger, and distortions of the 3rd Dimension. You have the opportunity to be a multi-dimensional being, participating in all levels to the 12th Dimension. All have this opportunity, but it will come slowly to some. It will require a 50 to 100 years for all to be in the 5th Dimension. Many who are lagging will not live to see this glorious event. On the other hand you can live to see it all; you can experience it all.

Time is collapsing. Will this make it any easier for those who are lazy to achieve 5th Dimension? Somewhat, however the same rules apply; self-discipline, dedication, and joy are required. Pay attention to your own development, and have fun doing so — for it is the grandest of adventures.

Know that your brothers and sisters from around the universe walk on this planet. Look into yourself and know who you are. Do not give your power away to others asking them to define you. Look inside yourself; everything is there. You can discover who you are, and enjoy that realization. Look inside and be grateful. Your heart will tell you who you are. Follow your heart — let your light and happiness shine forth for all to see. Then you will know who you are, and others will recognize who you are.

The new Earth will be a wondrous place, a 5th Dimension paradise that many from around the universe will wish to visit. It is slowly becoming a planet that has arisen from the darkness of the 3rd Dimension. You can have a role in helping to make this happen. Yes, you.

— Adrial 4-25-13

In Summary

Sedona, Arizona in the U.S. is known for its vortices. At the recommendation of a local resident, my wife, Heidi, and I stopped to visit the Airport Vortex. When we approached the trail sign, some unseen hand directed me to a trail along the side of the hill to the right. We had only begun to climb a short ways when an unseen force took hold of the front of my shirt and forcefully pulled me ahead. I was powerless to resist. I stumbled along the trail of red rocks and ruddy dirt, until the force evaporated. "Guess this is where I'm supposed to stop," I said to myself. From my perch, I looked out over a deep canyon. In the next instant a voice said telepathically, "Everything we have communicated to you will come to pass." As I type these words, I feel that everything is indeed happening, albeit not exactly as I had believed it would, but it is happening.

The communications I have received, both those posted and not, overall convey positive messages about the future of humanity and of our planet. Both my star brothers and sisters, and more recently Archangels and Ascended Masters, are telling us that the eventual ascendancy of Earth to a beautiful planet of light, love and unity is assured. There are enough lightworkers on Earth — souls who have incarnated for the express reason of assisting the transformation of the planet — plus ordinary humans who have awakened to see a better way of life, that there is no longer any question about our eventual positive outcome. This should be a great comfort to all who labor toward a 5th Dimension Earth.

As I indicated in an earlier chapter, I have ample evidence that extraterrestrials are visiting our planet. With the Sedona message and other communications I have received and am now receiving, I know that there is a much larger non-physical reality, of which I am a part. Furthermore, there is ample evidence that all of humanity has been subjected to intense off-planet influences, although most people do not accept this evidence, preferring to settle for reports of an occasional UFO sighting or a report of the appearance of an angel or saint. I have learned from experience that it is not just extraterrestrials who have been influencing Earth humans with communications, but those of the vast non-physical realm have also been quite active.

"The darkness has proven to be well entrenched" is a sentiment often expressed by those who are impatient with progress to a new Earth, and those who retreated after no significant event happened for them on December 21, 2012. While focusing on our personal development may seem like a slow process, as opposed to a single spectacular event, the creation of 3rd Dimension with its attendant effects took a very long time; it will take some time to fully dismantle it. Personally, I would not be surprised if it took fifty years or more for all Earth humans to pull themselves into the 5th Dimension. However, remember that time is collapsing, so maybe it will not seem so very long after all.

I now see that it is unwise to dwell on things that do not affect me directly, for doing so lowers my energy, particularly if I allow anger at situations to rise up within me. Our first responsibility is to care for ourselves and to love ourselves. We can best assist the rest of humanity by raising our individual energies, not by becoming embroiled in and angry at politics, monetary systems, corporations, religions, disasters and distant events. If we are earnest about removing the remnants of the 3rd Dimension from our planet, we must each walk away from all the manifestations of the 3rd Dimension without letting them impact us.

As individuals begin to behave on the basis of the 4th Dimension — love, connectedness, non-judgment and peace — governments and other structures will change to reflect these behaviors. This will eventually spread throughout the Earth; then the way will be opened for the rise to the 5th Dimension for more and more of us. I see evidence of the beliefs associated with the 4th Dimension spreading; now it is time to start behaving in line with those. Following that will come the knowingness associated with positive experiences.

The One

So-called channeled information is a valuable source of insights for individuals living in the density of physical form. As Mark has said, use discernment to find what resonates with your inner knowingness. We who provide information such as we are now doing do so with the intent to uplift you from the ordinary course of your lives. We trust that you will find our words of assistance.

The fall of consciousness occurred over a sector of the universe that encompassed Earth. It came about because some Creator Gods continued to create in ways that were not wholly according to the Prime Creator's grand plan of embracing Its light. When this happened, distortions began in their creations and the level of consciousness diminished. In order to save Earth from total annihilation through a loss of consciousness, a rigid density to be known as 3rd Dimension, was established by great beings of light, and further creations by those Creator Gods were stopped. Thus was Earth placed into the rigidness of 3rd Dimension.

Dark entities, with diminished light of Prime Creator, are the result of this fall of consciousness. These beings operate from fear, judgment and separation. They seek to dominate others in an attempt to fulfill what they are not. Grasping for solutions, they seek technologies to compensate for a lack of light. When their home planets prove unable to satisfy their cravings for light and love, they venture out into other star systems. Earth was headed down this path until December of 2012, when the underpinnings of the 3rd Dimension were removed and the multi-dimensional pathway was opened.

Periodically, Earth has been visited by entities from other planets in whom the light is diminished, as well as beings of the light from star systems untouched by the fall of consciousness. Both have interacted with Earth's humans, have formed alliances with humans, and have left their imprint.

Some of the descriptions of dark entities, and also of off-world beings of light, and even experiences with them, are the *products of fertile imaginations. Furthermore, some are contrived by humans wishing to enslave other humans by using fear of the strange and unusual. Moreover, all visits by off-world beings are easily interpreted as fearful if one is functioning from a fear-based rational mind.*

Chrysalis

6

Messages: Extraterrestrials
and Archangels

The following are summaries about others who have received messages and/or are currently receiving them from non-humans, either those of the non-physical realms and/or extraterrestrials. There are many others I have not included. I strongly recommend that you do not attempt to track all the channeled messages that are available. Use your discernment: Find messages that resonate with your heart and follow the posting from a limited number of sources. Then, if you find yourself not satisfied, at a later date you can always seek out different sources.

Eduard "Billy" Meier

Billy, a citizen of Switzerland, is the source of many UFO photographs in conjunction with the Pleiadians, beginning in the 1970s. He also has metal samples, sound recordings and film-footage. What we are interested herein is not verification of Billy's photographs or materials; I leave that to those with a scientific bent or a skeptical mind. Rather, we are interested in the messages he received from the Pleiadians as follows.

Billy's discussions with the Pleiadians are highly detailed and wide-ranging, dealing with subjects ranging from spirituality and the afterlife to the dangers of mainstream religions, to human history, science, and ecology, and additionally prophecies of future events.

"We, too, are still far removed from perfection and have to evolve constantly, just like yourselves. We are neither superior nor super-human, nor are we missionaries ... we feel duty bound to the citizens of Earth, because our forebearers were their forebearers ..."

— Semjase, Pleiadian cosmonaut

"General public contacts are not in our own best interests at this time and besides, they would not convey a correct significance for the state of mind in which we now exist."

— Semjase Pleiadian cosmonaut

"A single second in the timeless, amounts to many million years in normal space."

— Ptaah, Pleiadian cosmonaut

"We do not reach to the end of the universe, for such does not exist."

— Semjase, Pleiadian cosmonaut

"On many occasions space travelers have visited your Earth from other stars (108 different civilizations at last count), sometimes from very distant systems, like ourselves. On occasion, accidental contacts which are unique may take place with earth people."

— Semjase, Pleiadian cosmonaut

"A spiritually developed being, as a part of creation, acknowledges creation in all things, even the smallest microbe, and leading a creative life causes fears and doubts to vanish like rain before the sun.

"By creative thinking man acquires knowledge and wisdom and a sense of unlimited strength which unbinds him from the limitations of convention and dogma.

"Material life on Earth is only a passing event, a phenomenon van-ishing after a time. However, before him and after him there continues to exist the creative presence of the universe."

— Semjase, Pleiadian cosmonaut

Joan Walker

As a clear channel, Joan was chosen as the vehicle through which the many concepts of Level 3 were channeled.

Joan is a gifted channel for the Archangels and ascended masters and has used this gift personally for many years. She emerged into the public arena in 2005 as a channel and spiritual teacher by facilitating teachings and special projects for Master Kuthumi and Archangels — Metatron, Michael, Zadkiel and Uriel — to guide humanity's shift in consciousness. As a clear channel, she has been instrumental in the development of the "I Am Light Curriculum" and "Mastering Alchemy Level 2 and 3 programs." (I have had the privilege of knowing Joan for several years; she is an extraordinarily clear channel for both communications and energies.)

Joan is now guided to make herself known to all. At the specific request of Archangel Metatron, and under the guidance of the Archangels and Masters, she is now developing basic teachings that anyone can use in their daily life. For this, Joan and the Archangelic realm have enlisted the assistance of her life partner and husband, John Walker.

Following is a recent channel from Joan.

You can find other channeling, plus a wealth of material — programs and learning aids — at Joan's web site: www.joanandjohnwalker.com

Archangel Michael's Shield via Joan Walker

Greetings, beloveds, it is I, Michael.

I come to distribute to you three energetic templates of Light. These energetics emanate from the Godhead and are the specific components of a shield of light that we will co-create together. The first energetic component is courage. It is a frequency of light that is given to you completely and is available for you to use in this time of change. This energetic template of courage is available to you always as I hold it very firmly so that you might use it efficiently. Draw it in.

Visualize yourself creating with me, this magnificent shield of light that is both a receiver and a transmitter. There is a vibrancy that is created within this shield as the light is drawn into it. The energy of courage is an integral part of the radiance that is present. When you use this shield, you are able to face any obstacle that the fallen paradigm of fear exemplifies, and are able to dismantle it so that you can navigate your life from your Christed nature. You have the ability to face any obstacle. Breathe in the shield of Light, as I bring it forth to you at this time.

The second attribute of this shield is fearlessness: the ability to stand your ground, to hold your Light, to be the Christ. The image of the Christ is based in fearlessness. It is filled with Light and Love, which are never separate in their function, so there is never any whisper of "dominance over" in the fearless actions that you take in these times of change. Breathe in this great light frequency of fearlessness and make it a part of your make-up. It is part of your shield and is radiating the Love and the Light of your Source. When you are conscious that you hold the Love and the Light of Source, you can be fearless because you are powerful. Take it in. Breathe it in.

The third template of Light that I transmit to you at this time is the Love of Prime Creator. Love in this energetic template is an element of creation and is very powerful. As it shines into the mass consciousness of all humanity, it alters humanity's ability to transform its fallen state of consciousness. Take it in. Receive it. It is part of who you are; you have the power to create effectively because you are the Christed one who was created in the image of Prime Creator. You can create the changes that are required to bring this planet fully and completely into the ascension process. You can open the pathway to create a different experience in the world for many who are not as prepared as you.

When you transmit the light energies of this potent shield into the Earth and into humanity, you create a possibility for all those who are asleep or resistant to change to be influenced by the Light and the Love that you are emanating from your heart. This shield is a receiver as well as a transmitter of the Light and Love of Prime Creator. It enhances and magnifies these energetics, and helps you to distribute them fully everywhere you walk on your beloved Earth. Another attribute of this shield is that as it magnifies the Love and Light, it also reflects it back to you, so you will never again forget who you are as a Christed being, or the mastery that you hold.

Take in this radiant shield that you have been gifted with in this moment. You have all that is needed to navigate and create change in the world. But you must use it. You must center yourself in your Sacred heart and hold this shield firmly, so that this light is not only exemplified, but also consistently draws in more frequencies of light that are offered to you on a regular basis. Hold it firmly in the forefront of your energetic field. Display it so that you transmit it into all realms of form. I lovingly disperse these energies to you, to assist you in what you are called forth to do. ....

This channeling continues at:
www.joanandjohnwalker.com

Mastering Alchemy

Jim Self and Roxane Burnett co-founded Mastering Alchemy. As an international speaker and author, Jim has been leading seminars and teaching healing, clairvoyance and personal energy management courses since 1980.

Since childhood, he has retained a conscious awareness and ability to recall his experiences within the sleep state. Over the last twelve years, this awareness has expanded into relationships with the Archangels, Ascended Masters and Teachers of Light. The tools and information presented is a co-creation of these relationships.

Jim also walks well through the third dimension. At the age of 26, he was elected to his first of two terms to the San Jose, CA City Council and later became Vice Mayor. Before completing his second term, he was asked by President Jimmy Carter to be an advisor and the Director of Governmental Operations for the Dept. of Energy. Since then, Jim has successfully built and sold two corporations, and is the founder and current Board Chairman of a third. He loves to road-bike long distances and drink green smoothies.

Roxane is an author and teacher, and has been offering tools for developing intuition and Personal Power to individuals, businesses and women's groups since 1994. Following a successful career as an art director for two major corporations and as manager of her own design firm, she joined Jim and co-founded Mastering Alchemy.

Roxane's seminars include: Spiritual Abilities and Tools for Intuition, Personal Energy Management and Female Alchemy. She also has been featured on television, radio and in national publications both in the U.S. and Australia. She loves to dance and garden.

I first met Jim and Roxane when I was just emerging from my business life, had just published my first two books, and did not comprehend any of what I now know. The mind-expanding information conveyed, the exquisite energy infusions, and the unique exercises and creations in which Jim and the Archangels and Ascended Masters have involved me are truly outstanding. These have resulted in connections to all levels of non-form and led me to a better understanding of who I really am. I am unaware of any other program that provides this.

My goal for Mastering Alchemy has been to raise my consciousness while removing the baggage of my former life. To accomplish this, I have undertaken a daily meditation and experiential practice under the guidance of Jim, the Archangels, and the Ascended Masters. As I write these words I am activating my lightbody — something that has seldom been achieved in Earth humans since the fall of consciousness.

Lectures, books, videos, and messages, along with programs, are available at: www.masteringalchemy.com

Tom Kenyon

The following words are taken from Tom Kenyon's site: tomkenyon.com. I recommend that you investigate the wonderful experience of Tom Kenyon for yourself. His principal channeled messages are from the Hathors.

Neither the voice nor the man can be explained in one paragraph or in any combination of words. He is essence of, manifestation of, emanation of ... and his vitality, his magic and his integrity cannot be articulated in electronic swipes of ink on a papyrus of light particles captured on a computer screen.

There are those who say that one should leave one's sense of logic and rational thinking behind when entering into the spiritual realms of experience — that one must fully and completely surrender to faith and not let reason enter into the picture. Personally, I think this type of thinking is dangerous. We need all our wits about us and all the intelligence we can muster if we are not to become deluded on our way to spiritual illumination. It is the true light of self-awareness that we seek, not the false luminosity of personal fantasy and desire. In this regard, logic and rational thinking are not the nemesis of channeled communications; they are critical allies.

If I might be so bold as to summarize the Hathors' central message, it is this — as humans we have access to other dimensions of consciousness. This interdimensionality is part of our innate being, but it is something that has to be cultivated or developed.

The ability to access these higher dimensions or creative worlds within ourselves, although rather esoteric, offers unique practical benefits. For one, these other dimensions of consciousness can often reveal creative insights and solutions to problems that are not apparent in our normal ways of thinking and perceiving.

Tom Kenyon's web site is: tomkenyon.com

Patricia Cota-Robles

Patricia is cofounder and president of the nonprofit, educational organization "New Age Study of Humanity's Purpose," which sponsors the "Annual World Congress On Illumination."

Patricia was a marriage and family counselor for 20 years. She now spends her time freely sharing the information she is receiving from the Beings of Light in the Realms of Illumined Truth. This is accomplished through her weekly on-line radio program, web site, webinars, books, CDs, DVDs, email articles and free seminars.

Patricia's philosophy is: Every person is precious and Divine, regardless of how far his or her behavior patterns and life experiences may be from reflecting that Truth. We are not the victims of our lives. We are the co-creators of our lives.

Patricia's web site is: www.eraofpeace.org

Celia Fenn

Celia is an International Spiritual Facilitator and Channel. She works primarily with the Archangel Michael energy to bring information about the transformation and ascension of the planet, and the work of the Indigo and Crystal beings at this time. She holds MA and PhD degrees in English Literature, and has also studied Art and Music. She lives in Cape Town, South Africa.

She worked for 12 years as a University academic before switching to a career in Healing and Therapy. For ten years she helped many people to find their own personal healing path to wholeness and inner peace. She then became a channel for Archangel Michael. She is the author of *A Guide to Complementary Therapies in South Africa* and the e-book, "The Indigo Crystal Adventure."

Her current projects also include the interface between Lightworkers and the Indigenous people of the planet and their wisdom as a necessary part of creating balance and harmony on the Earth.

Celia's web site is: spiritlibrary.com/celia-fenn

Steve Rother

Steve lives in Las Vegas. He was an entrepreneur, until he became a Lightworker and an author. Five books have been published so far; they have been translated into eleven different languages.

His change from entrepreneur to Lightworker happened following a spiritual experience on New Year's Eve 1996. That night, he started saying things that, according to himself, did not originate from himself, but came from "The Group," a group of nine "energetic entities." These messages brought by The Group were bundled into books. Together with his wife Barbara, he travels around the globe, spreading these messages from the group and putting them into practice.

Steve and Barbara's web site is: www.lightworker.com

Geoffrey Hoppe

Geoffrey and Linda Hoppe founded the Crimson Circle in 1999 and have guided it to what has now become a global affiliation of New Energy teachers with the purpose of inspiring consciousness.

The Crimson Circle started in the living room of the Hoppes' home in the Rocky Mountains outside of Golden, Colorado. At the time, Geoffrey was an executive and co-founder of AirCell, Inc., an aviation telecommunications company. Linda was owner/manager of Sundance Group, Inc., a marketing consulting company. Geoffrey had been privately communicating with an Ascended Master known as Tobias for several years. As word about the Tobias Materials began to spread, the meetings quickly grew beyond their living room.

Linda and Geoffrey work closely together with Adamus or other Ascended masters to deliver their messages. As the channeler of the information, Geoffrey expands his consciousness into the non-physical realms and receives the "thought packets." He then translates the message into words for others to hear.

Geoffrey's web site is: www.crimsoncircle.com

Alex Collier

Alex is in contact with inhabitants of the Andromeda Galaxy and has messages from these visitors to Earth. Alex states that the Andromedans are of the Nordic race. His statements include an elaborate history of the Earth from his aliens' point of view. At one time, Alex had been forced into obscurity due to threats, but now is emerging into the public eye. Alex claims that there was a common language in the world. The common language was called "Tamil," which he claims was taught to us by the aliens. Tamil is now spoken in South India, one of the very oldest ancient languages.

Alex Collier's web site is: www.alexcollier.org

Barbara Marciniak

Barbara is an internationally acclaimed trance channel, inspirational speaker, and best-selling author of *Bringers of the Dawn, Earth, Family of Light* and *Path of Empowerment*, which collectively have been translated into more than twenty languages and have sold over 500,000 U.S. copies. She has a BA in Social Science, and is the publisher and editor of the quarterly newsletter "The Pleiadian Times." Her extensive worldwide travels, astrological studies, and a lifetime of alternative freethinking augment her personal understanding of the material she channels.

The Pleiadians are a collective of multidimensional spirit beings from the Pleiades star system, and have been speaking through Barbara since May of 1988. The Pleiadians are here to assist humanity with the process of spiritual transformation. Their distinctive style blends wit and wisdom, common sense, and cosmic knowledge in teachings that encourage expansive thinking and personal empowerment, and which have been compared to native shamanism.

Her web site is: www.pleiadians.com

Matthew's Messages

The evening of April 17, 1980, Suzanne (Suzy) Ward was packing for her next day's business trip when she received the call from Panama that changed her life: Her 17-year-old son Matthew had died after a vehicle crash that day.

The loss of a child had such an immeasurable impact upon the family that Suzy's preoccupation with Matthew's death would not be considered quite unusual. The direction she took in trying to cope with her grief, however, might be considered that. She called a medium with whom she had become friendly three years before, when they had lived in the same city, and asked about her son. The medium told her that he was in "deep rest"; she would receive an unmistakable sign when he was ready to send her a message, and when that time came, she would be led to a trustworthy medium.

The sign came almost nine months later in her first dream about Matthew since his death, and in the months that followed, she learned of three mediums; none asked Suzy anything except her son's name. They talked with her about Matthew, passing on to her what Matthew was telling them — the love between him and his mother was the inseparable bond that enabled him to be aware of her comings and goings. Matthew also told those who spoke for him that when the time was right, he and his mother would communicate directly.

It was early February 1994, almost 14 years after Matthew's death, when he started speaking to his mother. It was not simply her longing for this moment that created it — something definitely extraordinary was happening! For a while, each morning as Suzy recorded her and Matthew's conversations at the computer, along with feeling elated by this glorious development, she struggled with the thought that perhaps some bizarre part of her mind was emerging. Soon, though, she realized that her imagination could not possibly produce the astounding information she was receiving from her son and, by now, the entities whom he introduced to her.

It wasn't long before Matthew started talking about the books she was meant to prepare from their transmissions. He told his mother that her profession as journalist was not by chance; it was experience she needed so that, later on, she could properly work with the information he and the others would be giving her. But the huge task of reviewing, indexing, integrating and organizing months of daily messages into some logical order was a challenge she didn't care to accept, and she kept ignoring her son's urging her to "start the book."

Finally, he told her that her primary mission of this lifetime was to publish that information about life beyond Earth and the celestial advice and guidance urgently needed during this era of unprecedented planetary changes. Finally, he answered her question about why he had died at such a young age: He had to, so he could send her that information.

The web site for Matthew's Messages is:

www.matthewbooks.com

COMMENTS: In the prior chapter, I presented messages that I have received both from my star brothers and sisters as well as from Archangels. In this book, I am also presenting the words of "The One," a group of Ultraterrestrials. I have also presented backgrounds on and messages from other sources of channeled information. Now it is up to you to delve into all of these and determine for yourself what resonates with you. Look within to find guidance. Rely on your intuition to seek out the messages that are based in love. Immediately discard what produces fear or anxiety. Find what is right for you and then stick to it, for at least a while. Do not attempt to follow all the channeled information that is available from all the different sources.

In Summary

All of the channeled messages we have been receiving are directed to one purpose: To awaken us to who we really are. Channeled messages from both off-planet and/or non-physical beings provide us with information we could not obtain in any other way. The messages tell us about who we are, inform us about the lives of other beings on other planets, give hints about the larger picture, and explain the non-physical and non-form. I have found them to be an invaluable source of growth as I have matured into higher consciousness.

As explained earlier, I have also found that I can communicate with both off-planet and/or non-physical beings. For over sixty years I did not realize that I had this ability. Now that I have demonstrated it, I believe that everyone can do it; all you have to do is have the interest, believe you can do, and practice. So give it a try and let me know how you are doing.

Chrysalis

7

Earth History:
Extraterrestrials and Innerterrestrials

In my opinion the material in this chapter and the next is of critical importance because it will help you understand:
- The vastness of the experience in which we find ourselves
- More about who we really are
- Where Earth and her humans are headed

At the very least, this information may lead you to appreciate the planet on which you live, the scope of the physical universe and the many life forms who inhabit it, and the even more grand non-physical reality of which you are also an integral part. And maybe you will come to see that while individual change can happen quickly, change on a planetary scale takes quite a while.

It is not my intent to present an exhaustive review of all the varied accounts of the history of our planet, for that would take many more pages. There are many somewhat differing sources of Earth's history: Scientific (based on astronomy, archeology and geology), Religious (based on the Bible and other sacred texts), Innerterrestrial (those who live beneath the surface of Earth), Extraterrestrial, Archangelic, and other channeled sources.

In this chapter I present three somewhat differing points of view about the history of Earth and the universe. The first two of these are from the extraterrestrial viewpoint: The Andromedans via Alex Collier, and the Pleiadians through Billy Meier. A third viewpoint comes from the Innerterrestrials. In the next chapter is a fourth viewpoint from Archangels Metatron and Michael.

I will not present any history based on either current scientific theories or religions, as most readers are aware of these, or can easily discover them. So I leave you to decide which of the points-of-view, or combination thereof, appeals to you.

COMMENTS: The points of view presented hereafter give different time frames for historical events. This is due to the difficulty that non-Earth humans in different vibrations have with Earth's linear time, particularly for events that took place many years ago. (Linear time as we experience it was created to assist 3rd Dimension beings and that it is disappearing as we move into higher lighter vibrations.) I expect to learn more how these various points of view dovetail at some later date.

The Andromedan View

Alex Collier and Tolec communicate with the Andromedans. Only Alex speaks extensively about the history of Earth from their point of view. The following is from presentations he has given. I have received only general information from the Andromedans about Earth's history.

The Andromedans speak of an ancient race known as the Founders or the Paa Tal, who are said to possess engines whereby they can create matter, environments, and undertake terraforming to make planets suitable for all types of life forms. The results of their undertakings are planets with oxygen, hydrogen, methane and ammonia ecosystems, and the potential for sentient beings. They are also capable of relocating moons and moving planets closer and further away from stars, to change solar radiation levels. According to Andromedan archeological records, sentient life forms, reptilian, human, plasmic and methane, all appeared suddenly in full form, meaning they were brought from somewhere else. (*No explanation is offered as to where these different life forms came from. Also, it is important to note the vast differences between a race based on a hydrogen atmosphere and one based in oxygen.*)

The Andromedans say there is a "Creator," and that she is of a female frequency. They also say that 3rd Density is 21 billion years old, and that the universe, including all dimensions, is 21 trillion years old in Earth years.

During Earth's Paleozoic Era, 554 million years ago to 245 million B.C. (scientific definition), there occurred a dramatic explosion of diverse, multi-celled animals on Earth. All these showed up out of nowhere; no evolutionary process is in evidence. At that time, Earth was laying on its side compared to where we are today. Africa was at the South Pole; the West Coast of North America was at the equator. Suddenly, at 245 million B.C., 90 percent of all marine and animal life became extinct.

During that time, ET races developed space travel. The Alpha Draconians, the Ciakar, were the most technologically advanced, and the first to venture forth. Other races learned from them and also ventured into space, spreading their races throughout the Milky Way Galaxy and nearby Andromeda Galaxy. Those from Lyra, who colonized many oxygen atmosphere planets, were the distant ancestors of all human races. Soon, misunderstandings developed between the hydrogen and oxygen cultures, due to a variety of factors, including innate attitudes toward persons of other races. Eventually, treaties were negotiated between star systems and races, trade routes were established, and colonies were initiated to encourage the exchange of technology and ideas.

During Earth's Mesozoic Era, 245 million years ago to 65 million B.C., dinosaurs showed up on Earth seemingly out of nowhere. During that same time, Earth's vegetation underwent major changes. At the end of that period, an asteroid hit the Earth in the Atlantic Ocean, the dinosaurs became extinct, and the planet became much more friendly to human habitation.

During this same period, many planetary civilizations mastered space travel; by the end of this period, interplanetary trade had been established for over 17 million years. The most established star races, the Ciakar of Alpha Draconis, the Orion star civilizations, and the Lyra/Vega star systems were engaged in colonization. "Tubes of focused time" or wormholes, as Earth's scientists currently theorize them, enabled the star races to travel beyond the speed of light and to spread their cultures throughout the galaxy.

During this period, the star races were also transplanting vegetation and life forms to other star systems around the Galaxy that showed potential to support their particular form of life. Many targets were oxygen-based ecosystems because they are more desirable than other ecologies. Nonetheless, oxygen-based ecosystems, still numbering in the billions, are much more rare than hydrogen-based systems. It was during this period that dinosaurs, birds and fruit trees were transplanted to Earth, Mars and Uranus from other star systems.

During the Cenozoic Era, 65 million years ago to present, races from other star systems repeatedly visited Earth. At some moment during this period, a primitive race of humans emerged on the planet; the Andromedans do not mention their origins.

Nine hundred thousand years ago, the first self-contained bio-dome was established on Earth by the Ciakar along the New Mexico/Arizona border. This bio-dome was self-contained in that it provided all that the residents required: a hydrogen atmosphere, shelter, food and supplies. When the Ciakar went into the surrounding areas of Earth, they wore space suits.

A succession of expeditions/colonies were thereafter established on earth:

- 750,000 years ago the tall greys from Orion established the second bio-dome at Euromani, China.
- The star race of Capella, part of Ursa Minor, established their bio-dome in 740,000 B.C. at the base of Mt. Yogan in southern Chili.
- The Vegans, oxygen breathers, came next in 700,000 with a bio-dome along the Libyan/Niger border.
- The Cassiopeians, an entirely insectoid race, were next in 600,000 B.C. with a biosphere in Algeria, North Africa.
- The Nibiruans, hydrogen-breathers, were next with a biosphere in 580,000 B.C. in Cairo, Egypt.
- Orion sent a second expedition 90,000 years ago to Perth,

Australia.

- The Lyrans, oxygen-breathers, came back 80,000 years ago to the Basque area of Spain.
- Orion came again in 70,000 B.C. to Mt. Neblina on the Venezuela/Brazil border.

All of these colonies eventually packed up and went home, having obtained all that they wanted from Earth's ecosystems and inhabitants. Many of them were hydrogen-breathing extra-terrestrial races, and found their home planet less interesting than Earth with its complex ecosystem. Additionally, hydrogen-based beings tend to be much larger and slower-moving than oxygen beings, so their home planets were much different; their fascination with Earth continues to this day. In addition to studying Earth's complex ecology, some of the colonists attempted to genetically manipulate plants and animals to live in a hydrogen atmosphere.

In 72,000 B.C., Lemuria was founded as a collective colony among races from the Lyrans, Sirius A, the Pleiades, and Butuse, all oxygen breathers. In 58,000 B.C., the Pleiadians, the Nibiruans, Alderbarans, Antariaens, the Hayades and the Andromedans founded Atlantis. The Nibiruans were the only hydrogen breathers at Atlantis. In 31,000 B.C., Lemuria was destroyed in war. In 28,000 B.C., Atlantis sunk beneath the Atlantic Ocean.

The Pleiadian Viewpoint

According to Billy Meier, the Pleiadians participated in constructing the Great Pyramid of Cheops and the Temple of Hathor in Egypt. Inscriptions in the Temple and the orientation of the Pyramid with its inner chambers were left as clocks that are oriented to the rotation of the star system from whence the visitors came.

The earliest Greeks worshipped the Gods who descended to teach the arts and crafts of civilization to humanity. Many of the ancient Greek myths relate to the lives and adventures of these great divinities. Ancient Greek temples were constructed with an orientation toward the Pleiades.

In South America, the Incas built temples to worship their Pleiadian mentors, who had taught them to use fire and to plant and harvest crops. Machu Pichu in Peru is a stunning example of the connection between the ancient peoples and their off-planet ancestors. The Nazca Plains in Peru are also oriented toward the Pleiades, offering additional proof of the involvement of the visitors from the Pleiades. Couple this with the legends of the indigenous peoples of South America and one can fairly conclude that off-planet beings have been involved with Earth humans for many thousands of years.

At Teotihuacan north of Mexico City, the west face of the Great Pyramid of the Sun is oriented to the setting of the Pleiades, while the west running streets point to the same spot on the horizon. In the jungles of the Yucatan, the Mayan constructed temples at Chitza Nitza and Xwatinaya.

Innerterrestrials

I have compiled the following view of Earth's history from the innerterrestrial point of view for two reasons: It is different from extraterrestrial histories, and it opens a whole new line of inquiry into beings you may not know about. For those of you who are not already aware of the cities and peoples of Inner Earth, I am sure that the following will precipitate many questions. If you have further interest, I suggest you search the Internet; there are several good books available on Telos, the city beneath Mt. Shasta, and about other civilizations such as Agharta in Inner Earth.

Some of the survivors of Lemuria occupy Telos. It was constructed prior to the cataclysm of Lemuria; its initial population was 25,000 people; today it numbers one million. Its people are of a higher dimension than most Earth Humans.

The recorded history available at Telos indicates that the founding of Lemuria took place 4,500,000 years ago, when the first beings from the Land of Mu incarnated on Earth. These first beings lived in 5th Dimension light bodies. Earth at that time was the most magnificent planet in all of Creation.

Races from Sirius, Alpha Centauri, and the Pleiades came to Earth, joining those already here to form the Lemurian civilization. They colonized a huge continent in the Pacific Ocean. This continued until the fall of consciousness, which occurred over several thousand years, eventually causing all to fall to 3rd Dimension.

Thermo-nuclear wars took place between Lemuria and Atlantis at about 25,000 B.C. They had quarreled over control of the less evolved peoples of Earth. Ultimately, Atlantis and Lemuria became victims of their own aggression. About 12,000 years ago, Lemuria sank into the ocean. The only remaining pieces of that vast continent are Hawaii, the Easter Islands, the Fiji Islands, Australia, and New Zealand.

At the same time that Lemuria was sinking beneath the waters of the ocean, Atlantis started losing pieces of its continent. Within 1,200 years, nothing remained. The planet shook for 2,000 years after these catastrophes. What did not sink into the oceans was reduced to rubble due to earthquakes and tsunamis.

Some in Atlantis foresaw that their civilization was coming to an end. They ventured forth to interact with the Maya, the Egyptians, and other indigenous people, to assist in building pyramids and to carry their knowledge of the larger picture across the planet.

In Summary

The above accounts point out the long and varied history of interactions between extraterrestrials and Earth humans. There is little doubt in my mind that the various races who have visited this planet have influenced Earth humans, both genetically and energetically. I believe that today's Earth humans bear the results of the interactions that took place over an extended time.

Before reaching any conclusions regarding Earth's history based on the above accounts, I suggest that you read the following chapter. It will give you a different perspective.

8

Earth History: Archangels

In this chapter I offer the creation of Earth as told by Archangel Metatron, through Joan Walker and assembled by John Walker. Keep in mind that this information is from a being who witnessed and participated in the events about which he now communicates. I have conversed directly with Archangel Michael to clarify some of this material.

The history of Earth has taken a few billion years to get where we are today. Long before this current era, before there was a physical universe or other universes, Source expressed oversouls to more fully experience Itself. Archangels were created to assist in diverse ways in the various universes.

Later came Creator Gods with plans for universes within which they were to create. In this universe, the Creator Gods created first in the non-physical, and then later in the semi-physical, where they created planets, star systems and galaxies of much less rigidity than we perceive today.

After this had proceeded for some time, some of the Creator Gods in our sector of the Milky Way Galaxy began to create outside the grand plan of Source. They began to create beyond the full Light of Source, attempting to create in more dense energy. They liked what they could create without relying on the grand plan, and created more and more outside its blueprint. Over eons, this led to mutations of planets and beings. Star systems that had developed from these mutations outside the Light came into conflict. This resulted in planets blowing up and civilizations being annihilated. Other sectors of the Galaxy were not affected, but there was a concern that the conflict might spread.

A meeting between the Lords of Light, the overall supervisors of creation in form, and the Creator Gods of the Light was held. They decided to create a planet, using the Source's Christed Matrix, as an example for other planets to emulate. To do this, they created the Elementals and directed them to utilize the four elements of earth, air, water and fire plus the fifth element of love.

When Earth was first completed, it was in 12th Dimension energy form; it had substance but not physical form. Its semi-physical form was in perfect balance. It was at this time that the first human was created as an example for others in physical form to follow: a crystalline lightbody.

"The Christed Earth" existed for two billion years. It was the jewel of this universe, a place of such peace and beauty that beings from all around the cosmos came to it to experience what it was like to live in form.

Using Earth as an example, star systems that had been affected by the mutations picked up Earth's energy to counteract the distortions. Using Earth's powerful example, all of the mutated star systems eventually returned to the 12th Dimension.

A second decline started when some Creator Gods again experimented with new types of physical form. This time some of their mutations were set aside rather than being subjected to quarantine. Some of these mutations then went about breeding and interacting, creating entire civilizations without Creator's Light.

Meanwhile, beings from around this universe continued to come to Earth to experience beauty, diversity and quasi-physical form. Some visitors came from those star systems that had mutated, bringing with them mutated energy. Some who came from realms of the Light picked up mutated energy and took it back to their home star systems.

During this period, Lemuria was established on Earth in an area that is now the Pacific Ocean. Its residents were of a 12th Dimension vibration, were of quasi-physical form, embraced love and unity, and functioned as a closely knit collective. Its population was spread from Australia to California.

During this same time, Atlantis was a huge planet in a distant star system with very advanced technology. Its people were most intent on what it was they wished to accomplish by harnessing energies. This self-directed energy, particularly dominance, created issues on the planet; its people recognized that Atlantis was going to self-destruct because they had misused their creative energies. Not wishing their civilization to become extinct, they looked for other places to colonize.

They petitioned the Lemurians to establish a colony on Earth, promising that they would abandon their old ways. The Lemurians concurred, confident they could alter the culture and consciousness of the Atlantians to follow the 12th Dimension path of love and unity. At that time the Christed matrix was active and accessible. The Atlantians agreed to embrace love and unity as they learned to live among the Lemurians.

However, because the consciousness of the Atlantians had declined due to intergalactic conflicts, after several million years, they began to demonstrate their old habits of domination in experiments with energy and matter by misusing the elements of earth, air, fire and water. This created a huge disruption in relations with the Lemurians. Those Atlantians who wished to return to the old ways then left Lemuria to re-establish Atlantis on the other side of the planet. Earth was caught in two different states of consciousness.

Those in Atlantis who wished to function from positions of dominance began to hold the balance of power. Over millions of years the Atlantians experimented with energies and alterations of physical form. These experiments resulted in cataclysms such as shifting Earth's tectonic plates. Earth then experienced two very different states of consciousness.

Such actions of the Atlantians affected all on the planet. As a result, the consciousness of Earth plunged from 12th Dimension to 7th Dimension. The Christed Matrix was removed because

Earth could no longer sustain that energy of love and unity. Lemurians were unable to hold their higher energy and their continent sank beneath the Pacific Ocean.

Later, as a result of these continued attempts to misuse technology and energy, Atlantis plunged into the center of the Earth. As a result, Earth fell into lower and lower energies and was on its way to being totally annihilated due to tectonic plate shifts, massive earthquakes, huge tsunamis and pole shifts. Before this could take place, Earth was placed into suspended animation as a means of saving it from annihilation. No higher life forms remained; only single cells persisted. It required 500 million years to stabilize the planet.

The Lords of Light and Creator Gods finally determined that by removing Earth from suspended animation and placing her into 3rd Dimension, there would be a foundation from which it might be possible, one day in the distant future, to return Earth to a 12th Dimension Christed planet. Under careful direction, the Elementals reduced every-thing on the planet to 3rd Dimension physical form: stable, rigid, dense, and survival based. (Fear, violence, separation and judgment came later as individuals struggled to cope with 3rd Dimension.) Linear time was introduced to assist humanity in dealing with 3rd Dimension. At that time, there was no unity consciousness or love on the planet. During the ensuing years, the Creator Gods and beings from planets that Earth had previously helped to raise out of their problems began to work on ways to restore the planet. This process has been ongoing for 500 million years.

In order to handle the denseness of 3rd Dimension, the Creator Gods and the Elementals created the current human form, a carbon-based body. These early humans functioned as separate entities, so different from the way in which the beings of Earth had previously functioned as part of a collective. The ego became dominant. The brain operated at a mere fraction of its capability. There was little awareness of self and the soul was not heard. The chakras became dysfunctional. Since that long ago beginning, Earth humans have slowly evolved.

During this time plants and animals were also introduced in carbon-based form, and like the humans, they took on fear, separation, and other attributes of that lower density. It was due to this creation at lower vibrations that carnivores evolved, along with the food chain that we know today. (As I observe deer, birds and small animals in my back yard, I see in their collective consciousness the energy of fear, for they are ever observant of their surroundings and potential treats.)

There have been many attempts to restore Earth since it was placed in 3rd Dimension physical form. Beings from other star systems, those for whom Earth had acted as an enlightened model, came to help put the planet back together, came to help struggling humanity. They introduced technologies like fire and cultivation to the primitive humans. Beings from mutated planets came to take advantage of the primitive race of humans, twisting energies and the biology of Earth humans to their ends. Over the eons, there were earth changes as the Elementals reacted to various energies by altering the face of the planet. All have had an impact on what the human race is today.

Throughout it all, humans struggled to evolve, until today we are finally at a place where we can leave behind the 3rd Dimension and return the planet and the human race to the higher vibrations. Beings from the non-physical realms have incarnated to live among the human race, teaching us in accordance with our ability to absorb the larger picture and concepts of life beyond our daily struggle for survival. Beings from planets of higher consciousness have come to lend their light to the pending transformation.

Domination

The fall of Atlantis and the subsequent fall of consciousness and the establishment of 3rd Dimension on the planet did not erase the energy of domination that the Atlantians had brought to Earth. From an historical perspective, we see it in conquerors such as Alexander the Great and Genghis Khan. We see it in the emperor Constantine, who deemed it in his best interests to use Christianity to dominate the Roman Empire. The Catholic Church then ruled Western civilization for many centuries as its "infallible" Pope dominated.

We see the energy of domination in the colonization of the world by European countries following the age of discovery in the 15th Century. Although they did so in the name of Christianity, the explorers and later governors of the New World deemed it their right to conquer and dominate the "savages" they found in newly discovered lands. Domination is a principal energy obstructing higher consciousness. In modern times, the energy of domination manifests itself in the many ways individuals wish to have power over others.

First, most current organizations are structured to encourage this; those that rise to the top do so because they manifest domination. Military forces are all about domination. National boundaries are further manifestations of the energy of domination, as are all organizations intended to enforce separation, rather than seeing all of us as brothers and sisters, and seeking unity.

Second, in sports and other places where domination is valued, it is most commonly called "competitiveness" and is highly valued. Based on my understanding of domination, all forms of competition that are based on the intention to exercise power over others are contrary to higher consciousness. Games like hockey or contests like prize-fighting are clearly examples of competition based on power over others. There are other sports where competition is not necessarily linked to domination. Where do you see competition relative to love and unity? Is it a person's intention that manifests domination in sports, or is it built into the activity?

Third, in our everyday lives people practice domination when they withhold vital information, when they profess to be an expert and dominate a conversation, or when they bully others to get their way.

Fourth, in its most extreme form, domination results in domestic violence, rape, torture, and/or death. To put it very succinctly, if we are acting from the basis of love and unity, there is no domination.

I most recently incarnated in Andromeda; since this Galaxy was not touched by the Atlantis experience, I did not bring the energy of domination into this lifetime. However, I did learn to compete well enough to be successful in the business world; this is now fading away as I gain higher levels of consciousness.

In Summary

Four very different accounts of Earth's history! Things that stand out for me are the involvement by off-planet beings, both extraterrestrial and those in non-physical form, plus the very long time frames communicated by all of these. Little has happened to Earth swiftly, regardless of who has been doing it. Keep in mind as you read about the number of "visitations" by extraterrestrials that there were Earth humans present and that ETs interacted with them.

I have been told that the different time frames for Earth's history can only be explained by understanding that 3rd Dimension linear time is different from time in the 5th Dimension, which is different than time in the non-physical. Archangel Michael has stated that historical time relative to Earth, as reported by either extraterrestrials or those now residing in Telos, is based on non-linear time.

Having stated the above, I believe it is impossible to have the planet we have today, with the tectonic plates and oceans more or less firmly in place, if the continents of Atlantis and Lemuria had slipped beneath the oceans a mere 12,000 or 30,000 years ago. I can barely imagine the chaos of land and water that attended these two gigantic events. Plus, the geological evidence indicates a much longer timeframe in the past when things like this may have happened.

I favor the Archangelic view because it comes from those who observed the events described. I can only imagine how it required massive undertakings on the part of the Atlantians to disrupt the entire planet so that it verged on annihilation. I can envision a civilization completely caught up in itself and its misjudged capabilities, a civilization seeking to dominate all. I can see where the Atlantian imprint remains with us today in those who believe dominance is the proper way to behave.

The difference from what occurred in Atlantis versus what is happening today is that we are in a whole new situation based on energies coming to Earth from the galaxy, from Ultraterrestrials, and from ETs, the removal of the underpinnings of the 3rd Dimension, and the development of significant numbers of light-workers who are focusing their energies on transforming Earth and Earth humans.

There are numerous other accounts of Lemuria and Atlantis, each with its own dates, its own legends of who the residents were, their philosophies and religions, and how each civilization came to pass away. This demonstrates the confusion that reigns when the rational mind is involved in uncovering truth.

The view as reported from Telos is substantially correct when one considers that the souls of their distant ancestors may now occupy their current bodies, and display some of their former energies. They are committed to benefitting humanity, so we may see more of them in the future. If we take the Telos estimate of 12,000 years ago and multiple it by 83,000 (my number), we come to one billion, the number of years that the Archangels have given us for the demise of Lemuria. Keep in mind neither group is operating in linear time.

The material presented in the previous chapter represents the Pleiadians' benign influence. I find it very convincing that they were key to the construction of the pyramids and other structures. They are also actively engaged with us through communications and incarnations.

I believe the view from the Andromedans, as reported in the prior chapter, gives us some interesting insights into fear-based channeling. I also believe that it is somewhat distorted by a failure to take into account the overall benevolence of the universe outside this sector of the Milky Way Galaxy. I am told that dark extra-terrestrials do indeed exist, that they have interacted with Earth humans, and that wars have raged in outer space. I am also told that their influence on earth is no more.

Are benevolent ETs, including Andromedans, still involved with Earth? Yes, I believe so, based on my communications with those aboard Athabantian. Their observations of humanity come from off-planet individuals who are among us, as well as from individuals aboard the star ship "Athabantian." The Andromedans' involvement with crop circles, their attacks on dark ET bases, and their messages offer ample evidence of the continuing involvement of at least that race of off-planet beings. I believe some ETs are walking the planet, due to their human-like appearances while others have the ability to assume human form either as walk-ins or clones.

These accounts of Earth's history have had a huge impact on me, first because they paint the involvement of non-Earth humans in our history, second because there is such a long and involved background behind where we are today, and third because of the importance of this planet. This is so different than the history of a lone sphere somewhere on the arm of the Milky Way Galaxy, with which I grew up. I now have a totally different mindset than I did before uncovering these extensive histories.

A most important lesson to derive from the history of Earth as told by the Archangels is that the density and rigidness of 3rd Dimension was imposed on Earth by non-physical beings in order to save her from extinction. There was no evil intention behind this, no sinister motives on the part of anyone. It was a necessary step taken to salvage the jewel of the universe, with the hope that in the future she would return to her former glory. Now, after 500 million years have transpired, we are on the brink of making that happen.

I also resonate with the Archangelic view, *first,* because it dismisses the Big Bang and the actions of chance leading to our beautiful planet and our wonderful, complex bodies. I favor

Source's grand plan for the universe and the activities of the Lords of Light, the Creator Gods, and the Elementals.

Second, it explains why we are enmeshed in rigidity, separation and fear, and why we are unable to rise above it using 3rd Dimension thinking and techniques.

Third, I can now rise above other less grand explanations and see the loving hands of the Creator Gods. Now I understand even better how physical form is created from the non-physical.

Fourth, it sets the stage for our resurrection from the 3rd Dimension and return to existence on a fully Christed planet in the 12th Dimension.

And *finally,* I now see that the achievement of a Christed planet will require many years to move all of humanity to that uplifted state of consciousness; nothing of such a huge undertaking can be accomplished in an instant.

The One

From a universe perspective, all is in constant flux. Change is ongoing. The rigid form in which you live would cause you to believe that all else is like this. Nothing could be further from the truth; the vast universe beyond rigid physical form is fluid.

The creation of Earth as a Christed planet was greeted with great rejoicing in the non-physical collectives. Subsequent to that creation, many came to Earth to enjoy the experience of living in form, first in the non-physical form and later in somewhat lower vibrations. It was during Earth's degeneration into physical form, and its loss of higher consciousness, that we caused the bedrock of the 3rd Dimension to come into being. It was an abrupt ending to a downward spiral for this magnificent planet, but it was necessary to create a rigid stop to the plunge into oblivion.

Even in that long ago moment, we knew that one day Earth would arise again to resume its role as the stellar planet in the universe. It has been a long and tortuous journey since. Now we are on the cusp of returning Earth to its enlightened status. Now we can see a time in the near future when it will once again glow with a light of its own, and shine like a star in the firmament. We are most grateful to all who are now participating in this advance, for it is through the efforts of Earth humans that the restoration of Earth is possible. We applaud you and encourage you to persist.

Chrysalis

9

Self Discovery

There are now seven billion of us on this planet. Each of us has much in common with every other Earth human, regardless of socio-economic status, race, physical size, sex, health, ancestry, age, education, job, wealth, power, religion, sexual preference, physical ability, geographic location, addiction, wisdom, and/or level of consciousness. Our home planet has a very diverse environment, animal population, minerals, and plant life; it is the most diverse of any planet in our Galaxy. Despite our diversity, Earth humans are more similar to each other than we are different. It is our humanness and our commonality of beliefs and behaviors that result in the collective consciousness of the conventional paradigm.

Our physical bodies are unique to Earth; we may resemble humanoids from other planets, however our physical make-up is unmatched anywhere else in the universe. Our physical bodies were created at the time the planet was placed in 3rd Dimension. Since then, they have been genetically and energetically manipulated by a number of external beings and energies; since then, we have evolved as a species known as the humans of Earth.

Earth humans currently live in physical form, an energetic construct that is characterized by density, rigidness, and polarity. Violence, separation, fear, and deceit derive from those and appear to be integral to life in the 3rd Dimension. Even those who live in a higher vibration are still surrounded by physical form and the remnants of the 3rd Dimension; their beliefs and behaviors are influenced by it both consciously and unconsciously.

I am aware of injustice perpetrated against individuals, races, and societies. I am aware of well-intentioned people who struggle to correct these injustices, using the lower vibration tools of the 3rd Dimension. I am aware of the wealthy and powerful and how they ignore the plight of the poor and hungry. I am aware of politicians who vote for the interests of those who provide money rather than those who elected them. I am aware of scientists and doctors who cling to outdated beliefs, despite evidence to the contrary. I am aware that in general individuals are ignored as the wealthy and powerful and their institutions impose their desires on those whom they deem to be ordinary. I am aware that there are a small number of Earth humans who are wed to the 3rd Dimension because it benefits how they experience their lives. I am intellectually aware of all these things; however, I do not engage them or allow them to impact me emotionally.

I am aware that the majority of Earth humans operate in the 4th Dimension — where fear is not at the root of their lives. Not all see themselves this way, of course, but most do. Most people are trapped in the boxes of their upbringing, and most have carved out reasonably comfortable lives, despite their restrictions. A few Earth humans function in the 5th Dimension all the time, others part of the time. There are a small number of enlightened humans scattered about the world who are lightworkers and wayshowers.

Against this backdrop, *the most important thing we can do in this lifetime is to discover more about who we truly are, appreciate and integrate that knowing, and then act as who we believe and know we are.* I am convinced that all Earth humans will eventually become beings of 5th Dimension consciousness, and that Earth will rise to a much higher frequency. But first let us figure out who we are.

Each Earth human is intimately connected to an oversoul; a minute part of that oversoul has dedicated to his or her physical body during this lifetime. Our oversouls were created in the distant beginning of all. Our oversouls will live forever. We each have had many, many thousands of past lives, both in the physical and the non-physical. We each will have many, many more life-times.

From this perspective, we are each a great being of Light with physical form, non-physical form, and non-form aspects. We are magnificent and powerful. We are very complex beings while, at the same time, we are unified.

We each came here under a contract that was signed by our soul prior to incarnating in this body; a body intended to serve a specific set of objectives. That contract foresaw the life we would lead in this body, whether it is a life of relative ease or one of severe distress, whether we are wealthy and powerful or poor and powerless. This contract foresaw the parents to whom we were to be born and our siblings, as well as others with whom our soul would arrange experiences. It anticipated the particular "box" of beliefs and capacities into which we would be trained. And it anticipated whether we would come to realize who we are and whether we would allow that fact to be recognized by others. Finally, it foresaw our exit from this body.

No Earth human is completely untouched by the remnants of the 3rd Dimension, for we navigate within it daily. In most cases, our connection to it is unconscious because it is the way in which we grew up. The vast majority of Earth humans currently cling to the familiarity of the 3rd Dimension, whether they are happy or not, whether they are comfortable or not, whether they are wealthy and powerful or not, whether they sense that things are changing or not, and whether or not they are consciously or unconsciously functioning in the 4th Dimension. The 3rd Dimension is what is familiar and few are willing to change, or to walk away from it. There is a small fraction of humanity who realizes that change is inevitable, but sees change as impacting their wealth and status. These have dug in their heels to perpetuate the conventional paradigm.

Several important functions of the body were altered when humans were created to exist in the 3rd Dimension. This was done in such a way that eventually humanity could evolve to a state where all could return to the higher dimensions, and these functions would be integrated once again. The functions that were curtailed include the brain, chakras, glands, organs and blood. In addition, our soul was disengaged; not removed, but separated to wait reuniting. Each of us needs to upgrade these in order to achieve life in the higher dimensions.

Since Earth has existed in physical form, many extra-terrestrials from throughout the nearby universe have visited and interacted with us. Some of the interactions with these ETs have been to the benefit of humanity; some have not. Our physical bodies show the residuals of these interactions. Earth today does not resemble what she was eons ago, before the fall of conscious-ness. Earth humans today do not resemble what things were like when our 3rd Dimension bodies were first created by the Creator Gods. Over the past half million years, we have evolved to where today: We are now able to hold higher states of consciousness.

At the same time that extraterrestrials were visiting Earth and leaving their mark on humanity, great beings of light appeared among us in physical form. We know them as Jesus, Buddha, Saint Francis, etc. They, too, left a mark on humanity.

Based on communications from the Archangels and Ascended Masters, I have come to learn that the physical bodies of all Earth humans are changing. Some are changing faster than others, depending on the individual's attachment to fear. Many who are receiving similar information believe our physical bodies will turn into some sort of "crystalline" form. My information is that our bodies will become quasi-physical — very fluid — as we become "physical bodies in higher dimension consciousness." We will have to wait for this to occur, for I do not believe we will see quasi-physical bodies mixed with conventional bodies as this would be too disconcerting — like having extraterrestrials of odd forms walking among us.

Beyond this revelation, I have been informed by experiences in the non-physical that my soul is both vast and comprised of many facets, and I now see my body is a small fraction of who I really am. After raising my current consciousness, with several years of effort, I now function as an individuated Divine Being of Light in a physical body. All humans of Earth have the ability to achieve this physical/non-physical body/soul construct; however, most are completely unaware of it, or deny it, due to their conditioning and beliefs.

We are receiving energies of light that are gradually altering our physical bodies. This is a gradual process as the human body can only absorb these very powerful light energies slowly. In time, all of humanity will be transformed, but it will take a very long time unless other factors become involved. To absorb these energies more quickly requires an intention to receive them, a high level of awareness, and an almost daily focus.

My Non-physical Self

My physical body is a very small portion of who I am, compared to how huge my non-physical self is. I have somewhat separate mental and emotional bodies that are much larger than my physical body. I have fourteen chakras that are not part of my physical body, but are closely attached to it via the etheric body. My oversoul is both vast and eternal, having been expressed in the first moments of creation; it has many parts, each with a slightly different function. Its various "aspects" are both closely allied with my body and attached to Source. It contains my higher mind, my higher self, and memories from other lives. My oversoul is vast indeed, for in simultaneous time it is carrying on thousands of lives in physical form, and many more in non-physical form. My oversoul is larger than I can imagine, for it is in both form and non-form, an even vaster arena of consciousness.

Only in form — physical or non-physical — are there individual energies and individual personalities. The purpose of form is to foster unique expressions. A very, very small percentage of form is physical, and then only in this universe. Other universes also have form, but it is not like the physical form that is in this universe. Source is exactly what the name infers: It is the initiator and upholder of these many universes of form and non-form.

Some people say, "I am God." To me, this diminishes the beauty and wonder of creation, and correspondingly shrinks who I am. To me, the word "God" refers to the Creator Gods who created this physical universe. Source is much, much more, because the physical is such a small portion of this universe. Plus, most people have no knowledge of the many other universes and the vastness of form and non-form within each. The totality of our physical universe is much less than one percent of all.

I have experienced some of the vastness that is beyond my physical form. Words cannot adequately express its wonder and beauty. Therefore I say, "I am not Source; I am in unity consciousness with Source." To me, words are important and I use them to describe everything as precisely as I can.

I have experienced unity, or oneness; my experiences are beyond words to adequately describe. I have experienced unity with animals and trees. I have experienced unity with my star brothers and sisters, as well as my Earth human brothers and sisters. I have experienced unity with the Ultraterrestrials, even though I cannot comprehend the vastness of who they are. Do I remain in unity at all times? No, I have not yet attained that level of consciousness; I find myself going in and out of unity. Yet while I move in and out of perfect unity with all, I never lose sight of the fact that I am an individualized Divine being of Light in a physical body.

My physical body is a precious vehicle through which my soul experiences uniqueness. My soul experiences uniqueness in all of its manifestation of form in the non-physical. That is the reason for form: To express uniqueness. I believe that we should honor our uniqueness because there is a reason for it. Honoring our uniqueness does not mean we are separate from Source, only that we honor Source's ability to be all things, including unique. Understanding these concepts gives us a new reference point for understanding who we are.

Is Source within me? Of course, for I have both physical and non-physical aspects of who I am, and spirit is definitely an aspect of who I am. Saying, "I am in unity with Source" is an immense concept, for it expands who I am. Am I in unity with my soul? Again, yes, for my physical body is a minor manifestation of my soul. I believe these are important distinctions.

What I am conveying here is that each of us is a gigantic being of Light, an eternal expression of Source; but we are not the TOTALITY of Source as the words "I am God" would imply. We are both in unity with Source and unique. I am a unique manifestation of Source in a physical body. I may be playing with semantics here, but I believe that words are important, particularly when describing a relationship of this importance.

Recent Events

On November 11, 2011, the Christed Matrix — that had been removed from the core of the planet at the time that it became evident that Earth was tumbling into lower vibrations — was returned to the Earth. This action was taken, based on the events previously described that led the Archangels, Creator Gods and Lords of Light, who had observed Earth humans for eons, to see that humanity had reached a state of evolution that Earth could now be returned to a Christed planet. This action was undertaken along with the cooperation of hundreds of highly conscious Earth humans.

Furthermore, in conjunction with this momentous event, a tiny Christed Matrix was installed in each Earth human. Regardless of their status or situation, each received the same Christed Matrix. This has made it much easier for everyone to now move into higher vibrations.

On December 12, 2012, the energetic construct that had been holding 3rd Dimension in place was removed. The same celestials who had implemented 3rd Dimension in the first place did this. Again, this was done in conjunction with highly conscious Earth humans. What this means for each of us is that the foundation upon which the structures, relations, beliefs, and deceits of 3rd Dimension were built are no longer in place. What remains is the momentum of millions of years of being mired in the 3rd Dimension. What has now become evident is that those people who cling to the features of the 3rd Dimension — fear, violence, wealth, and power — are now becoming desperate to preserve what they have in the 3rd Dimension, and to hold to that in which they feel comfortable. In desperation, they are ratcheting up their efforts to hold onto what they have.

On December 21, 2012, nine days after the energetic construct of the 3rd Dimension was removed from Earth, the path was opened to allow all Earth humans to achieve multi-dimensional existence. This was extended to all physical beings beyond our planet, to the solar system, to the Galaxy, and to the entire universe of physical form.

There were many who looked upon the Winter Solstice of 2012 as a magic event. Those of a scientific bent saw Earth passing through an alignment with the center of the Galaxy and an ionic cloud, all of which was supposed to create significant earth shifts. Needless to say, the earth shifts did not occur. Those who were focused on extra-terrestrials thought that this moment would be the time of the mass landing, when all would be taken aboard starships to avoid the collapse of the planet. While not giving up on the rescue scenario, they were quite disappointed. Others believed that the economy and/or the government would undergo significant changes, again focused on the magic date. Once again, to those viewing everything from a 3rd Dimension perspective, nothing in the physical realm has changed much as a result of December 2012.

My perspective, and the perspectives of other Earth humans of higher consciousness, is that changes did occur. The changes were not of a physical nature; they were within the non-physical of each individual. From that December 2012 moment, it has been easier to observe events in the 3rd Dimension from a non-involved perspective. From that moment, it has been easier to concentrate on raising my vibration using any one of a myriad of techniques.

Integrating

Take time each day to focus on the following. I have been at this full time for over eighteen years; I still do not totally appreciate or realize what it means to be who I am. This new vision is so different from the 3rd Dimension in which I grew up that each day is like a renewed awakening to a realization of more vast and beautiful ways to see myself.

First, we have been told that Creator Gods, using Source's grand plan, created the physical universe — all that we see in the night sky and through our telescopes.

Second, there are billions of other planets with sentient life forms and that these are our brothers and sisters. Trillions of beings with physical forms that may or may not resemble ours!

Third, these other life forms from out there are also here, in their starships and walking among us. The humans of this planet have interacted with them! Extraterrestrial contacts have left indelible imprints on all of us.

Fourth, Earth humans interact daily with beings from the non-physical: Angels, Archangels, ascended beings, and Ultra-terrestrials. For most people, these interactions are unconscious, but they need not be.

Fifth, Earth once existed as the jewel of the universe, a planet so beautiful that beings from all of creation visited to experience her. At that time she was a Christed planet, holding a 12th Dimension radiance of love and beauty.

Sixth, Earth experienced a fall of consciousness as Creator Gods experimented with ever more dense forms of creation in this sector of the Milky Way Galaxy. 3rd Dimension was established to prevent Earth's annihilation.

Seventh, Earth existed for billions of years before she became physical, and then another billion years as 3rd Dimension was put into place. Humanity has a history of at least 500 million years. We cannot equate linear time with time in the non-physical.

Eighth, there are recent events (11-11-11, 12-12-12, and 12-21-12) that portend a very different future for each Earth human. With these events we see the return of the Christed Matrix, the removal of the underpinnings of the 3rd Dimension, and the path to the higher dimensions made available for all in physical form.

Ninth, an oversoul placed a fragment of itself within each of us to be here at this time and place. Our souls are both complex and unified, non-physical and non-form, eternal yet present in every moment. Our souls are having many, many other lifetimes both in the physical and in the non-physical. Our physical bodies are much less than one percent of all that comprises our souls.

Tenth, we are great beings of Light having a physical experience. When we see ourselves from our souls' perspective, it is like being the driver of a vehicle.

Eleventh, do not diminish life in this physical body. Enjoy the natural things of this planet, enjoy food, enjoy interacting with other Earth humans, and enjoy and honor all our experiences, our thoughts, and our emotions as Earth humans.

Twelfth, the most important thing we can do in this lifetime is to discover who we are, appreciate who we are, integrate that knowingness, and then act in each moment as who we really are.

Take a little time each day to reflect on the above twelve points. What do they tell you about who you are? Take time to dwell on all twelve points. For a moment think, "What if all the things Mark is telling me are true? Not just one or two of the above, but *what if they are all true?*"

It is okay if you can only accept one or two of these at this moment. It has taken me eighteen years to accept all as true. But ask yourself, "What if all are true?" Think about who you are in that context: You are a great being of Light experiencing life in a physical body.

Where will this lead you? No one can predict. We are each on a very individual journey, both in the physical and in the non-physical. I encourage you to undertake your journey against the background of all that I have outlined. I have not regretted my journey; I am sure you will not regret having reached out to experience the greatest experience of all: Self Discovery.

The One

Discovering who you are in a human body is a most important task for you to undertake during life in this body. Once you know who you are — a physical vehicle under the control of an eternal soul — you see your life much differently. Know that your soul is expressing itself in many realms at this moment, for it functions in simultaneous time. From your soul's perspective, you are its most important lifetime for it is you who will influence all of creation. Pay attention to this wondrous revelation, for you are powerful beyond your imagination. One of the principal benefits of knowing more about who you are is that it dramatically reduces fear in you.

One cannot know perfect unity with Prime Creator until one has experienced the many expressions of Prime Creator. Yes, you are Divine beings in a physical body; however, there are many, many expressions of Prime Creator, both in form and in non-form; all are one with Prime Creator. We Ultraterrestrials are expressions of Prime Creator; we are of form and non-form; we are each unique while a collective, and one with all.

Chrysalis

10

Levels of Consciousness

In this chapter I am offering my personal ascension to higher levels of consciousness to illustrate how anyone, even a conservative old businessman, can function at a 5th Dimension consciousness, at least some of the time. On the following pages you will find some rather amazing things that happened to me on my way to this place. Is it necessary to experience all of these? No, I know many others who are happily in 5th Dimension consciousness without undergoing experiences with extraterrestrials and communications with non-humans such as I have had. I see it as my hard headedness, or perhaps my comfort with things of the lower dimensions, that made it necessary for me to undergo my attention- getting experiences.

Something within is calling each of us to discover who we really are and why we are here at this time and place. This is not an easy task given the conditioning we have been given: 1) by our parents, siblings, and playmates, 2) by our teachers, priests, ministers, rabbis, bosses, and coaches, and 3) by the national media, books, and movies. As a result of the fall of consciousness, we were created in rigidness, polarity and separation to enable us to function in 3rd Dimension.

I believe that 99 percent of the conditioning that I grew up with was not true. The "box" in which I functioned as a child was quite small with rigid sides to constrain me into the beliefs and patterns of my Catholic family. My adult box consisted of the conservative attitude of a financier, a distancing from things of the heart, judgment of others as different and somehow not acceptable, and a self-involvement about not doing something wrong. Is it any wonder that I was reluctant to change and focus on strange new ways of seeing things that did not relate to what I had known? Am I blaming anyone for putting me in my boxes? No, for they all were simply living out what they had been taught.

When I was functioning at this, my lowest level of consciousness, I was enveloped by fear around money, status, and the future. I had been programmed from a very young age to believe that I was supposed to be a success in the world of business and technology. I eventually became a successful venture capitalist; in doing so, I paid scant attention to anyone or anything that did not further my advancement or my instant gratification. I struggled with who I was. I struggled with trusting others. There is a saying in the world of venture capital, "Even your best friend will try to suck you into a bad deal to save himself." To be realistic about how I behaved during this time, I was in a state of reaction, unconsciousness or fear much of the time. *This level of awareness is 3rd Dimension consciousness.*

During that period of my life, I had a wonderful career and a marriage that resulted in two great sons — of whom I am proud and whose families I very much enjoy these days. During my years at 3M Company, we conceived the idea of the magnetic striped credit card. I left 3M to join a small company that pioneered the first swipe reader for credit cards and the first currency dispenser (ATM). During my days as a venture capitalist, I funded the first pulse oximeter — that has become a standard of care in medical facilities around the world. So I relate to those that tell me the world, as they know it, is a pretty good place. And I recognize that they may have carved out a very comfortable existence within the conventional paradigm.

At the same time that I was enjoying great success in my business career, my private life was falling apart. After divorcing my first wife, I went through several years of consuming alcohol and enjoying the company of different women. My connection to things of a higher consciousness became almost non-existent.

Once again, I can relate to those who are having experiences like this. From my current perspective, I respond to all that I now realize that I can be so much more when I am not focused on material comforts and pleasures. I am grateful for all the assistance I have been given to help me get to where I now am.

Returning to that moment in my life, it was not until I decided to really look at myself that things began to change. 1996 was the year when a most wonderful, beautiful woman came into my life: my wife, Heidi. Without her consistent love and support, I would not have been able to continue discovering who I am. That same year, I walked away from the world of business because something within me said that it no longer served me; I resigned from all Boards of Directors, stopped reading business plans, and lost interest in following the latest technologies. The business partners of my earlier venture funds had seen it coming as early as 1990 and mutinied against my leadership in 1991. They no longer saw me as "the eagle with the blood on its beak." Looking back, I now see what a gift that separating from the business world has been.

I was to find out years later that three beings had come to me in 1987 to tell my higher self that it was time to do what I had volunteered to come to Earth to do. My energy changed as a result of that encounter, and I began to present myself differently. That is what my former business partners had picked up on. Looking back at my life as a venture capitalist, I must admit that I really enjoyed the benefits that a huge salary and perks provided. I now see it as shallow, but at the time it was one of the best careers offered.

Not long after I resigned my career in business and finance, I went back to school to get a Master's Degree in Psychology. I had several experiences in the months studying for my degree. First came a gut-wrenching period delving into what I believed, and how I saw my environment and myself. Through the eyes of experienced social workers and psychologists, I saw the socio-economic situation in the United States from a whole new perspective. I saw how people of privilege looked upon those of a lower level, or those of a different race, as basically unworthy, lazy, and less than fully human.

I saw a small number of people at the top of the pyramid, those in positions of power and wealth, for whom the 3rd Dimension worked quite well. I had dealt with them in the business world, and now I recognized in them an arrogance of which they were most likely unaware. I realized that I had once had some of that same attitude, but something within me had prevented me from adopting an elitist attitude, and I had finally left it behind.

About that same time, I learned about secret societies that had no intention of acting in humanity's best interests, and dominated institutions like banking, government and corporations. During my internship, I became aware for the first time in my life of the vast numbers of people who "put up with" the conventional paradigm because they knew no other way. I encountered families that were broken and battered. I encountered people with addictions to substances and violent behavior. Through eyes of compassion, I saw mental illness. And I came to understand that the same soup of everyday life surrounded even those who were more enlightened.

My awakening to the reality behind the conventional paradigm was a real eye-opener. I sought a place of refuge. I collected food and other supplies in anticipation of a massive collapse of society. I bought gold and silver coins to hedge the collapse of the monetary system. I became distrustful of my fellow Earth humans, judging them to be so asleep that they could not see the disaster that was coming.

I came to see that the vast majority of people were part of a system that had never worked to their benefit. And I came to appreciate that love expressed by those "in love," between parents and children, between brothers and sisters, and/or among friends, was a cherished commodity; it did not extend to society as a whole because the larger society was based on separation, competition, domination and fear. At the same time, I abandoned the last vestiges of the Catholic religion in which I had grown up. Nonetheless, I still retained guilt, fear, separation and judgment as the controlling factors of my life, but recognized it consciously rather than operating at an unconscious level. *I view this somewhat awakened state as low 4th Dimension consciousness.* I have been told that the majority of Earth humans now operate from this level of consciousness.

It was after my awakening in 1987 that I accepted the reality of other beings beyond the confines of my box, beyond the limits of our planet, and for the first time saw off-planet beings as something other than science fiction characters. This changed how I saw myself: I was a humanoid along with many others in the universe. At this initial awakening, I did not see them as my brothers and sisters; rather they were strange creatures whom I regarded as aliens and feared.

As I was working on a paper for my psychology degree, a story poured out of my computer: A story about ETs who were wandering among us, trying to inspire us to awaken. It also included narratives about a secret government. It captivated me. I had considered becoming a psychotherapist, but my passion became the book. I journeyed to Australia to study Family Therapy under Michael White. After two weeks, he counseled me to follow my passion, "finish your book." I then opened myself to what the book promised, and labored over it until it was ready to be published.

As the result of that first book, I slowly emerged into a slightly higher consciousness — I found myself open to contact with extraterrestrials and sought out the Center for the Study of Extraterrestrial Intelligence. In 2001, after a week near Crestone, Colorado with this organization, I was in shock. My consciousness took a dramatic leap forward: Not only were there physical beings on other planets; their ships and other phenomenon were here for me to see. My level of fear subsided as I began to see the larger picture, and how I was part of it. I went home to finish my first book, *Trillion,* with only minimal revisions as a result of actually seeing UFOs. This experience in the Baca Grande had blown away more of my views based on the conventional paradigm, and set me firmly on a path that has led me to where I now am.

If there are any of you reading these words who doubt the reality of ETs, I suggest you spend a week with CSETI: www.cseti.org/ambassador-trainings.html

I now felt that I had a mission: To tell others about what I had seen and how it had affected me. I wrote the *Paradigm Trilogy* to express what I knew. My consciousness had advanced another step. It was then I knew that the media, government, and science were covering up the truth about this larger picture, as well any number of other things. *I was now at mid 4th Dimension consciousness:* 1) Realizing the extent of the universe and knowing that it is populated by other sentient beings. 2) Knowing there were many things that were being kept secret from people by those that wished to dominate. 3) Reducing my fear because of what I had seen. 4) Recognizing that I was operating from a higher state of consciousness.

However, I did not yet realize that most of the universe is benevolent and that only this sector has been subjected to the fall of consciousness. Nor did I understand about the vastness and power of the non-physical. I was able to set aside my fear of darkness after a week of seeing ET phenomenon, and felt strangely open to what would come next. From CSETI I did pick up concerns about the many secrets ordinary people are not told in order to control them, and I heard predictions about gigantic earth shifts and added them to list of concerns.

In 2008, when my friends from Andromeda approached me about communicating their messages and posting them on my web site, my old ways of seeing things took a back seat. I began to see myself as the fortunate recipient of knowledge from a more advanced civilization. I began to see that I was to dedicate my life to exposing the larger truths communicated by them. Another realization came into my consciousness: These beings were my star brothers and sisters; they were not so vastly different, just a step more advanced technologically and spiritually. Their messages were about the ways in which they saw Earth humans trapped in 3rd Dimension rigidness, domination and fear, and how there was a grander way to live, a way that embraced love and oneness. I migrated to this place after a few months of engaging with them. My fears about Armageddon abated. Even though they said they would not come to save us, I now knew that they were here to show the way. *Yet I was stuck in the middle of 4th Dimension consciousness.*

It was at this point that my star brothers and sisters "suggested" a new way to advance my consciousness: Mastering Alchemy. As I look back on the transition to interacting with Archangels and Ascended Masters, I can see the wisdom of their suggestion. I also see that it was where I began functioning from my "higher mind." I also see that my interactions with my star brothers and sisters set me up to take full advantage of Mastering Alchemy and interacting with Archangels and Ascended Masters.

After four years of following a daily regimentation, my consciousness has taken giant leaps forward. I no longer have anything to do with the 3rd Dimension and its separation, fear, lies and violence. *I spend most of my time in the 5th Dimension, where I can experience the non-physical.*

Most recently, I have become aware of the arena of the Ultraterrestrials, that vastness of non-physical beings in multiple universes, most of whom have never heard about Earth or physical form. Now I have no fear. I have been told that my soul is living thousands of simultaneous lives. Now I comprehend that I am part of a great being of Light, an exceedingly small portion of which is attached to my physical body. I have been told that my body is precious and that many other oversouls wanted to utilize it to be here at this time and place.

I have been told that my recent lifetimes prior to my current life were on a planet in the Andromeda Galaxy. I have been told that I agreed to come to Earth at this time and place to be a part of the restoration of Earth as a Christed planet of love and unity. And finally, I believe that we, Earth humans, have been tasked with returning Earth to its glorious status as a Christed planet of unity and love.

Now I see myself as an Individuated Divine Being of Light, and as a wayshower that emits an uplifting Light to all with whom I come into contact. My non-form is a part of the collective that embraces All There Is. I now know that I am in unity with everyone and everything in the cosmos, physical and non-physical, and know that my every thought, every emotion, every word, and every action are connected to all. Because of this, I have been told that to be part of the Love and Unity of the 5th Dimension, I must control each of these in every instant.

My Andromedan brothers and sisters tell me that I am now as spiritually advanced as any from Andromeda, and more conscious than many off-planet beings from the Milky Way Galaxy. I am now able to communicate with the Archangels, Ultraterrestrials, and extraterrestrials who are assisting me in writing this book. I have been told that I am slowly achieving lightbody status. And I have achieved such a close integration with my soul that I now see death as a choice to give up my current physical form, know that I can live as long as I wish, and believe that I can decide when to lay down this body.

Many people understand that each of us is undergoing a process to turn our carbon-based body into "crystalline." My understanding of this is that it will eventually result in higher dimension consciousness in a body that is quasi-physical. (Think of water versus rock.) I believe that it is an intentional process on my part and I am pursuing that path; whether that is true for you, I do not know. Nor do I understand how or when all of humanity, each individual Earth human, will ascend to higher consciousness in semi-physical bodies. I do know that wayshowers who have achieved higher states of consciousness are breaking ground to make it easier for all.

This is so different from where I used to see myself: First, as a man with minimal spiritual attachment, climbing to the top of the business pyramid within the conventional paradigm. Second, when I saw other Earth humans for exactly who they were — in their beauty and darkness — and when I saw myself as a human who was in a gigantic universe full of other physical beings. Third, when I was communicating with my star sisters and brothers. Now I see myself as a being of Light, having experiences with Archangels; now I believe that I have a grasp of who I really am.

I look upon myself as one emerging from a cocoon. I have not yet completely left behind the chrysalis to become the butterfly of fully higher consciousness.

I invite you to come to a similar realization. I am most grateful for where I am this day, particularly compared to where I was a few years ago. If I can make such a 180-degree change, so can you. Now that I have broken ground, your path will be much easier.

In Summary

Find a path to higher consciousness that fits your particular needs. Am I anyone special? No, I do not see myself as that, for I know many others who are of a similar consciousness, and I believe that anyone can come to this wonderful place, if they are motivated. Have I been given the beautiful gift of communication? Yes, I am grateful beyond words. I see myself but a step beyond where many people find themselves.

Some of my illustrations of the 4th Dimension involve an intimate association with extraterrestrials. This is not a requirement to advance your consciousness. I am most grateful for my involvement with my brothers and sisters from Andromeda, for they have helped me reach where I am today — without their help, I would not have done so. Is such an awareness part of your path? It may or may not be part of your journey to higher consciousness.

I once again express my gratitude to my lovely wife, Heidi. For she keeps me grounded so that I can ascend to higher dimensions and write while still functioning in this physical world. She came into my life at the moment of my transition and has stayed for 19 years.

You have the ability to do it your way. There are many paths available to you. Open yourself and one will present itself. There is a vast universe out there, be playful about all of this, no telling where it might lead you.

Greetings, Mark.

It is I, Moraine, communicating with you from the starship "Athabantian." I am here on behalf of those who you will recall communicated with you a little while ago, some of whom are your friends from Akima.

I communicate today to say that we are most proud of what you have accomplished in the human form of one who is on Earth. You have successfully moved from one who was mired in the 3rd Dimension to one who is now mostly in the 5th Dimension.

This has not been an easy transition for there were aspects of the 3rd Dimension that were very enticing and served you well, despite the overall sense of fear and uncertainty with which you were constantly plagued.

We are most happy to see you now in a place of peace and happiness. We hope you will recall that this was much the same consciousness that you had in your recent lifetimes on Akima.

Now we will watch with great interest to observe where you will go from here. You have several paths before you, all consistent with your newfound consciousness.

We wish you the very best on the next part of your journey; know that we are here to support you energetically. At some point in the future we will be with you, once again, in physical form.

Our blessings to you, and to Heidi.

11

Personal Transformation

Since those long ago days, when primitive humans were created by the Creator Gods and the Elementals, Earth humans have struggled to evolve themselves ever upward. There are many notable examples of this, such as the discovery of fire, the wheel, and the compass. We have been told that our star brothers and sisters assisted with these innovations as well as agriculture. Many non-physical beings have incarnated to contribute their knowledge and nudge humanity ever upward. Throughout this long period, a few enlightened people have spearheaded the advancement of consciousness in each age; they were those who saw a step beyond the conventional paradigm of their day. Let us look at a few recent examples of humanity's upward progress.

Greek Culture

Classical Greek culture of the 5th to 4th centuries B.C. is considered to be the seminal culture that provided the foundation of modern Western Culture. It had a powerful influence on Roman life. The Romans carried a version of it to many parts of their Empire. Greek philosophy had a major impact on raising the consciousness of humanity.

Christianity

Jesus brought the Christed Energy to Earth; his activities led many early Christians to pursue love as the foundation for a higher way of living. In the 4th century the Council of Nicaea codified the life and teachings of Jesus into the New Testament.

Under Constantine, Christianity became the official religion of the Roman Empire. Christianity has since spread throughout the world, and has, despite historic violence on the part of some followers, done much to uplift the consciousness of humanity through its emphasis on Jesus' message of love. Christians believe that Jesus is the Son of God, fully divine and fully human, and the savior of humanity. In my conversations with Jesus, he communicated that he came to Earth to bring the Christed energy; he did not come as a savior. Although he did not achieve all that he desired, Jesus' presence on Earth has had a profound effect on raising our consciousness.

The Renaissance and Exploration of the New World

The Western World looks at the period beginning in the 1400s as its awakening. This period, known as the Renaissance, began in Florence, Italy. Various theories have been proposed to account for its origins and characteristics: The social and civic peculiarities of Florence at the time; its political structure; the patronage of its dominant family, the Medici; and the migration of Greek scholars and texts to Italy following the Fall of Constantinople. The Renaissance is best known for its artistic developments and the contributions of Leonardo da Vinci and Michelangelo.

This was also a time of great exploration. It started in the early 15th century with Portuguese discoveries in the Atlantic and Africa. These were followed by the discovery of America by Columbus in 1492, Magellan's voyage around the tip of South America in 1498, and by a series of European naval expeditions across the Atlantic and later the Pacific.

However, according to recently discovered information, these events were preceded by the Chinese, who undertook voyages of discovery as early as 1421 with a vast armada of 50,000 men and women who circumnavigated the globe. In 1434 they instigated the Renaissance in Europe with the knowledge they brought to Florence. Their voyages of discovery landed in the Americas fifty years before Columbus; they supplied a map upon which both Magellan and he based their voyages. The small ears of corn in many Chinese dishes are the result of the maze that these early Chinese explorers brought back from the Americas.

Regardless of the particulars of this period, it marked a turning point in the evolution of civilization for both West and East, and an opening of a larger physical world than had previously been known and a new level of consciousness.

Democracy

The separation of the American Colonies from England and the establishment of a democracy (technically a republic) marked another major advance in humanity's climb to higher consciousness. Although the United States has moved away from the promise of what was established at that beginning, and has fallen under the influence of those who advocate fear, violence and domination, Americans still have the basics of a democracy. Other countries around the world have emulated the democracy found in the United States, albeit with somewhat different structures. Democracy, although not perfect, is certainly an advance in consciousness, compared to most other forms of government in place on this planet.

Abolition of Slavery

In the United States, the issue of slavery caused war between the States of the North and the South. While the ostensible issue was freedom for the slaves of the South, the real issue was economic. With the freeing of the slaves, upon whom the South's economies had been built, Southern plantation owners faced financial ruin. In other parts of the world, the abolition of slavery occurred at different times in different countries. These actions marked a new level of consciousness within humanity, as well as a new economic order.

Women's Rights

Recognition of rights for women and girls has taken many years. In some countries, these rights are now institutionalized or supported by law, local custom and behavior, whereas in others they are ignored or suppressed. Issues of women's rights include: bodily integrity and autonomy, suffrage, holding public office, working for fair wages or equal pay, owning property, entering into legal contracts, and possessing marital and/or parental rights. These fairly recent actions demonstrate another stage in the raising of humanity's consciousness. I personally believe that the way a society treats women is an accurate measure of that society's overall consciousness.

Environmental Movement

Encompassing scientific, social, political and environmental issues, this movement's principal tenets are the sustainable management of resources and stewardship of the environment. It recognizes humanity as a participant in ecosystems, not the enemy thereof. It does not condone the domination of the planet and its ecology in order to benefit those who own land. The movement is centered on ecology, health and human rights. The environmental movement is an international movement, represented by a range of organizations, from the large to grassroots. The fact that it is international in scope, involving all of humanity in a single issue, is another major step upward in consciousness.

A Critical Mass

Viewing events such as described above, the Archangels, Lords of Light, and other great beings of the cosmos have determined that humanity, after 500 million years, has finally established a track record, and developed a critical mass of enlightened beings. We have been assured that we now have sufficient numbers of lightworkers and wayshowers so that we can restore Earth as a Christed planet. The choice to follow through with this is now up to those of us who see the path ahead.

Personal Transformation

Now that we know more who we are, what can we do with the larger picture, peace of mind, and self-assurance that we now possess? My answer is to recognize that we have transformed ourselves and integrate that understanding so that others may experience our energies.

After that, we begin the process of further raising our consciousness to achieving a 5th Dimension consciousness while in a physical body. This means that we can further comprehend and embrace various aspects of our souls, and that we remake our physical bodies to accommodate the higher vibration while experiencing perfect health. Once we have achieved this, we may retain our bodies for as long as we wish — no more need to die. This is not something that will happen automatically; we must make an effort to achieve this state of being.

Everyone is constantly radiating who he or she is, both consciously and unconsciously, both physically and non-physically. It is time to take charge of what we radiate, and show who we really are. By this gentle process (gentle to ourselves and to those around us), we can influence others with whom we come into contact, influence them to want to have some of what we have. At all times, be sure of what you are radiating before trying to intentionally influence another.

We each have a personal energy field that surrounds us at about an arm's length. We can use it to consciously observe every-thing beyond ourselves as apart from ourselves, and avoid becoming unintentionally entangled with others directly or through the media, books and conversation. We can use it to define who we are in personal conversations, so that others learn to appreciate our energies and find that they cannot interfere with the real me.

The goal of our lives is not to achieve ascension and leave Earth; rather the reason we came here is to achieve love and unity with the planet and ALL who inhabit her. I see myself as giving my energy 100 percent to help open others to know what I understand, to experience what I have experienced, and to move all humans of this planet from being stuck in lower consciousness to truly living in the elevated energies of the higher dimensions. All of this is taking place beyond the "understanding" of my rational mind, as it will for you, if you too decide to pursue this higher road.

Whether we realize it or not, we volunteered to come here to assist with the return of this planet as a Christed planet of love and unity. To accomplish this, we will assume a new form, a fully Christed lightbody that is in unity with all; then we will function as 5th Dimension beings in physical bodies. By achieving lightbody status, we will help to transform other Earth humans, the Earth herself, and all in physical form.

The above may seem like a tall order; it was when I first encountered it. However, let us examine it one piece at a time, so that it may become more realizable.

One, focus on who you are in every moment. Continually remind yourself who you are as you go about your daily life as an observer. Learn to "walk tall" through the remnants of the 3rd Dimension without becoming attached to or involved with any of it.

Two, learn to control every thought, every emotion, every word, and every action in every moment. This may seem like a lot at first, but as you manifest higher vibrations, it becomes increasingly easier.

If you fall away from these two ideals, just head back to them as soon as possible. There is no guilt or blame associated with a miss-step here or there.

We are very powerful beings. Once we learn to focus our energies for our own uplifting, we can then direct them to the uplifting of all, not just on this planet, but everywhere in the physical universe. If this strikes you as something you wish to do, then find ways to make it happen.

It will take time to completely shift all Earth humans into the 5th Dimension. This shift will be the sum of many, many individual choices, with many, many people realizing who they really are and choosing to live out the reason they came to this planet. In all of this do not forget time, for as we begin to function in the 5th Dimension, linear time is collapsing and a different time is manifesting itself.

What about individuals who are stuck in the conventional paradigm? What can anyone do to convince them that there is a better way to live, and to give up their comfortable lives? The answer is that there is very little anyone can do to convince anyone else — a child, a brother, a sister, or a friend — to turn his or her back on the conventional paradigm. That is why it is taking so long to transform this planet — most of Earth's population accepts where they are.

It does not matter whether someone is wealthy and powerful, or whether he or she is poor and miserable, it is hard for anyone to open up to the unknown, to change, just because someone else says so. However, do not despair, everyone on the planet is receiving massive amounts of energy from the Galaxy and from all types of off-planet beings, energy that will both enlighten and make it easier to find the path to the higher dimensions.

There is a way that does not involve convincing anyone about a better life. That way is by using our energies. Here I am pointing out, again, that each of us emits energy from ourselves each moment of the day; without focusing, it is scattered. Have you been in a group when one person uplifts everyone? This is due to that person's energy overpowering the energies of the individuals in the group. We are very powerful beings; we need only learn to focus our energies.

Personal transformation may sound simple, and, yes, it is. You have only to make a decision to do it, and be open to what shows up. As in my case, ways will be presented for you to advance your consciousness. It really is that simple. And remember, each of us has his or her own path. Find yours, and stick to it. The results are wonderful beyond words.

If you have absorbed the words of this book, you have made great strides toward raising your consciousness. You now understand more of who you are relative to the grand picture of the physical universe. You now understand more about the non-physical as it relates to you individually as a soul/spirit with a physical body, and you have begun to comprehend the vastness of the non-physical of which you are an integral part. Now if you wish to move to yet higher states of consciousness, you must delve into that understanding that goes beyond words, you must experience the non-physical.

The One

Sooner or later, you will come to understand who you really are: An individualized aspect of Prime Creator in a physical body. This realization may be quite startling or it may only be uncovering what you now know to be true. Then you will view your fellow human beings in a new light, for they, too, are like you. No more will you see them as different, regardless of their behavior or beliefs. They, along with all the other beings in your world, in physical form, and in the non-physical, are manifestations of Prime Creator.

One of the principal benefits of knowing who you really are is that fear will be reduced. It may not immediately leave you, but as you become more and more comfortable with your new self, fear will disappear. Then you will notice all the wondrous aspects of the others in your life, on the Earth, and in the universe. For the first time, you will see others clearly, just as you now see yourself clearly. Once fear is removed, you are then free to explore more of who you are, and to ascend to greater and greater consciousness.

12

Planetary Transformation

As I stated in earlier pages, the transformation of humanity into the 5th Dimension will take a while — it could take many years, then again maybe not. In the meantime, most of us live in the 4th Dimension, transitioning individual by individual, into a higher consciousness for all.

As I observe progress toward transforming humanity, I see many people admitting that things are changing, and opening themselves to explore what comes next. They may not, as yet, have decided what to do about all this, but they are waking up. And I see more and more dedicated wayshowers who are stepping out to deliver their versions of what the new Earth will be like and how to get us there.

At the same time as the Light elevates its impact on all, I see people who are determined to stay the course within the 3rd Dimension elevate their efforts. I see political clashes and the influence of money into the political process at record highs, I see the calls for increased military and police action, I see religious fervor intruding everywhere in attempts to protect its turf, and I see the media trumpeting all these old values. Their influence can be considerable for those who are unsure who they really are. The best way to deal with such influences is to focus on love and unity for all humans, and on the Light of Source — and turn off the TV and be discerning about what you read.

I have also encountered people who have stepped back from awakening because they see change and the larger reality as too confronting — what they already know seems safer. Nonetheless, the Light continues its uplifting influences. It is important for us to support those who are struggling with the question of who they really are, why they are here, and what the future holds.

I am quite convinced that politics will not solve the problems inherent in the conventional paradigm, for politics is the art of compromise. Compromise by its very nature leads to perpetuating the old rather than courageously venturing into new territory. In the lower level of the 4th Dimension, politics is usually skewed in favor of the wealthy and powerful, particularly when money is allowed to have undue influence.

Military action and police presence solves nothing because using force to replace one powerful figure with another invariably results in but a different version of what the military action had been designed to do away with.

Although most religions can be credited with good deeds, they will not solve the ills of the conventional paradigm, for religions by their very nature suck energy from the people and place it in the hands of the few who wish to dominate through dogma.

Technology will not solve the problems of the conventional paradigm. While some of it is worthwhile, much of it plays to comfort and an unwillingness to take responsibility for actions. Plus, it can draw us further and further away from a connection to the planet, to things of nature, and to the basics of life.

Money will not solve the problems of the conventional paradigm, for supplying riches to all would do little because people without a focus would spend it in ways not in their best interests, while others would seek to accumulate it for their security or for domination over others.

I foresee that the political and monetary systems, as well as all other man-made structures, will undergo massive changes on the way to dismembering the conventional paradigm. I predict difficult times as we transform from depending on the stability of 3rd Dimension institutions to learning how to live with the increasing fluidity of the quasi-physical. I say this not to create fear, but to emphasize that knowing who we really are is all-important at this time of transformation.

The only lasting way to move away from the conventional paradigm is by creating a path based on love and unity. It is within the purview of the individual to take responsibility for his or her own life, to change by stepping into unconventional ways of creating, and to do for each other what the whole is unable to do for its collective self.

If we include knowing who we really are into the transformation equation, we have a very powerful way forward. If we can find others to join us on this path, together we can completely remake this world so that it no longer depends on politics, military might, money, religion, technology or manmade structures. We can create a world where individual Earth humans functioning at higher consciousness are the focus of everything. We can create a world of butterflies.

I believe that the only way to create lasting equality among people (after all, we are Divine beings in physical form) is by creating totally new ways of being, not just extrapolating the old order. First, we must go beyond this to recognize that we are powerful beings who are capable of communicating and creating totally new ways of being.

In the past I believed that we could move into a new way of living based on making adjustments to our current societies. In other words, I believed that the human species was capable of creating a new way of living, based on what was good in what we had, and then extrapolating to the new. The very idea does not involve a radical departure from the current.

I now see things differently. We will move to a whole new way of being: Beings with a 5th Dimensional consciousness in physical bodies, then in semi-physical bodies as we ascend beyond the 5th Dimension, and eventually we will be living on a quasi-physical planet with quasi-physical animals and plants. When we move from the rigidness of the 3rd Dimension to the fluidity of the higher dimension, our bodies and Earth cannot be termed physical by our current measures, nor can those who cling to 3rd Dimension rigidness survive.

Once we have accepted who we are as great beings of light, and then have transformed ourselves into powerful creators of our own experiences, we can work with the Elementals to transform Earth into a 5th Dimension planet. We do this by acknowledging the Elementals as the creators of the physical form of Earth and then projecting our positive energies in conjunction with them as they restore Earth to higher consciousness. Yes, we are that powerful. It does not require all of humanity to undertake this task, only a significant number of dedicated lightworkers. Each day we are getting closer to the critical mass required to transform all.

Having experienced the non-physical, I believe that we will create a new way of being on Earth, a more fluid way of being with a much higher consciousness. It is much more than merely changing a few troublesome areas to create a new civilization. I believe that we are quite close to having the necessary collective power create a new Earth of the 5th Dimension. To quote a Hopi saying, "We are the ones we have been waiting for."

EARTH SHIFTS AND EXTREME WEATHER: Communications from our star brothers and sisters, coupled with genetic memories of distant traumas, predicted huge earth shifts, land masses toppling into the oceans, new continents emerging from the waters, oceans moving onto lands that had not been submerged for a million years, and the entire face of the planet rearranged. These predictions included volcanic activity that would displace millions, tsunamis that would inundate coastal regions, and floods sweeping away cities and countrysides. These predictions have infiltrated the consciousness of the conventional paradigm, compounding fear of natural events. Because I was operating from a lower consciousness at that time, I incorporated some of these events into the *Paradigm Trilogy*.

I now see that ideas about extreme earth changes are, to some extent, memories of the fall of Atlantis and Lemuria. Just as the people of Telos recall the fall of Lemuria from their soul memories, we are recalling very old traumatic experiences through our soul memories and projecting them into current time.

I now foresee that such catastrophes will be avoided, and that we will ascend to a higher consciousness without massive upheavals. However, Earth will continue to throw off the remaining aspects of the density and fear that were imposed upon her. I believe that there will continue to be some extreme weather, forest fires, volcanoes, tornadoes, tsunamis and floods, along with extreme dryness, but nothing compared to what was previously predicted out of fear. As we humans ascend to higher vibrations, we are losing our fears, and we are already favorably impacting Earth.

My own behavior has changed as a result of my new understanding. Previously, I had sought a "safe place" to reside, away from any massive incursion of ocean waters, flooding, or volcanic activity. I had relied on the Hopi prophecy that the Four Corners Area of the United States was somehow a protected region, and I found a place to live within that region. I now see that my earlier behavior was not in line with who I understand that I am. I have moderated my old behavior, but I still store some food and essentials, not totally depending on the local supermarket to have what I want.

EXTERNAL ENERGIES: The Andromedans say that their starships, and those of other off-planet beings of Light, have been beaming positive energy to the planet for the last 60-plus years. Other than communications from our star brothers and sisters, and channelings by others, I have no experience with these historical efforts. On the other hand, I have no reason to doubt them; I have repeatedly been told they are true. In addition, it is my experience that many non-physical beings are projecting energies to assist Earth humans to raise their energies.

Earth is becoming warmer; the scientific evidence is convincing; only a few dispute it. Glaciers and Antarctica are warming from beneath, indicating a non-conventional explanation for the phenomenon of global warming. Still there are many theories as to its cause, from natural cycles to manmade. Our star brothers and sisters insist that humanity is not totally responsible. From the Archangels and Lords of Light we learn that Earth is warming because it is the recipient of massive energies from the sun that is, in turn, receiving energies from the center of the Galaxy. Earth is like a giant capacitor, storing these energies and causing the planet to warm from within.

This does not mean that the fouling of our air, water and land is a good thing, because it is not. Our off-planet friends insist that we do not appreciate how badly we are harming our beautiful home. From an energetic standpoint, our abuses will need to stop, and then be cleansed, in order to support Earth's transformation.

Before Earth underwent its long period of suspended animation, it was twice the physical size it is currently. The density of the 3rd Dimension caused her to shrink. As she returns to her former self, and assumes a semi-physical state, Earth will expand in size. This will cause shifting and restructuring. We have been told that the energies we are now putting forth with regard to Earth's return to a Christed planet of light will mitigate and make unnecessary any huge dislocations; however, those Earth humans in rigid physical density will no longer be able to live on the planet.

INTERVENTIONS: Sirians, Pleiadians, Andromedans, Arcturians, and great beings from other star systems continue to be involved with Earth humans. I have experienced their phenomenon and received their messages, as have others. They continue to insist that they are here to assist us, and to coach us in what we can do to wake up and influence what is happening around us. They insist that their starships continue to beam light to Earth, and they say that they are engaged in defending Earth from intrusions from outside, as well as eliminating the remaining dark entities. As I have said before, no extraterrestrial race is coming here to save us.

Archangels and other beings of the non-physical continue to communicate with lightworkers and wayshowers. Though their messages are interpreted differently, and their methods for achieving higher densities diverse, their overall messages and methods are more similar than different. Rather than depending on written words, take time each day to go within, for everything you need to know is there. Beings from the non-physical will speak to you in your dreams, in your awakening moments, and in your quiet times. Learn to listen to your quiet inner voice. There are many resources available to assist you; search them out.

In Summary

By recognizing who we are individually, and by joining with others of like knowing, we can change the civilization of Earth. However, it is not enough to base the new civilization on the old. By recognizing our power and our energetic influence, and by committing to use them to completely change the conventional paradigm, we can change the way we currently are operating, to a condition of love and unity for all.

New Earth

Many of the projections of what the New Earth will be like are coming from people who have limitations due to their backgrounds and worldviews. In my lower vibration of ten years ago, I wrote and posted about how we could reinvent our institutions, reform the monetary system, do away with fossil fuels, and move to a more open society, thereby transforming our current civilization into a more harmonic one. Some of those who wish to retain what works for them in the 3rd Dimension embrace this approach.

I now understand that this is not the path ahead. I see that as the 4th Dimension plays out, and as more and more people climb to the 5th Dimension, we will need less and less of what keeps us rooted in the physical. I see that within a short time, in universe terms, Earth will function as a 5th Dimension sphere.

These two visions are incompatible. The majority of humans on this planet are now functioning in the 4th Dimension, whether they realize it or not. Many people are now approaching 5th Dimension functioning, and some are living fully in it. Then there those who are playing out the density they embraced as part of the 3rd Dimension. We will continue to see conflicts as the two perspectives exert their influence. Energies from these two groupings influence the transformation of Earth. Those of higher consciousness advance it; those of lower consciousness retard it.

I see a time of transition before a majority of Earth humans live as described above. In the 4th Dimension we will still have need for food, water, shelter and transportation while focusing on achieving greater consciousness to bring about peace, happiness and beauty. Again we must do this without losing sight of the ultimate goal while walking in the current paradigm.

Because I see a completely new Earth human, radically different from the old, there is a part of me that wants to look beyond the 4th Dimension, ignoring the transition to the 5th Dimension. I already see men and women who are less and less physical. Although they may still appear physical, they have acquired lightbodies of the 5th and higher Dimensions. They are more boldly conscious, having put aside death and living in their bodies as long as they wish. Picture everyone in perfect health, without the fear of death. Once you have integrated this picture, you will radiate energy to transform many, and you will assist the energies of a new Earth.

I have been shown how the wondrous transformation of humanity will unfold, but not the timing thereof. We must first believe that we can move from our current consciousness to much higher levels. When I say *we*, I am talking about all Earth humans who decide to take this path. Then I see a completely new society based on love and unity. And last, but not least, I see Earth radiating her light and the light of her humans for the entire universe to view. This result is a transformation of an extraordinary nature.

Earth has now passed the tipping point. The Christed Matrix has been installed in her core; it awaits further activation by the energies of Earth humans, in order to envelope all in love and unity. Earth will be returned to her former glory as a shining example for all in the universe. Under the guidance of the Elementals, and with our continued focus of energies, she will shed the remaining influences of the 4th Dimension and grow to become a semi-physical sphere of love and unity. Then, as the consciousness of her humans expands, she will travel to the 12th Dimension.

In Summary

Ultraterrestrials, extraterrestrials, and innerterrestrials, as well as those who have previously incarnated on Earth, have long waited for this moment: The transformation of Earth and her humans. Personal transformation is available to all of us. It is the process of uncovering who we are, integrating that knowingness, and then behaving accordingly. Societal transformation is happening all around us, one individual at a time. We can assist the transformation of all other Earth humans by our example of living in love and unity, and by purposefully directing our energies at all times. With the assistance of our energies, Earth is being transformed. Planetary transformation will lead to a 12th Dimension, fully Christed planet, and to the return of the Earth star.

1) We are immersed in a vast reality with many other
    beings, physical and non-physical. It is larger and more
    complex than human imagination can conceive. It has
    been here longer than imaginable and will be here
    forever.

2) We volunteered to be here at this moment of Earth's transformation. We are the ones doing the transforming. No one is coming to do it for us, or save us; it is up to us.

3) The transformation of Earth will not happen quickly. However, the transformation to a planet of love and unity will happen.

4) We are individualized Divine beings of Light in physical bodies. Our non-physical self is many times greater than our physical. We are powerful enough to transform ourselves into higher consciousness and to transform Earth.

5) Others may appear to be trapped in the murkiness of a chrysalis. By raising our own vibration, we can emerge as butterflies.

The One

Do not make the mistake of assuming that your civilization will continue to function as it has in time past. Your old way of life will be severely interrupted as everything moves to a higher state of consciousness.

Let us look forward to a very different world, a world of love and unity. It is to here that humanity will ascend, for this is the Christed planet that was once the original Earth. This is the planet that many have been working toward for hundreds of thousands of years, ever since the fall of consciousness. Yours is the planet that will set the stage for a universe-wide resurrection into the Light.

You Earth humans are the key to making this come to pass. For you see, we of the non-physical realm cannot create in the physical; it requires physical beings like you to return Earth to its former glory. So it is that we are here coaching and encouraging you to be all that you can be: Individuated Essences of Prime Creator in Physical Form. From this realization, and then a further realization of your non-physical aspects, you will come to understand that you have the power to transform Earth. Yes, you have the power through your intention, actions and determination to accomplish what others have failed to do. You can recreate a Christed planet as was ordained by Prime Creator eons ago. We stand ready to assist you in whatever way we can. Blessings.

Chrysalis

Acknowledgements

I would like to acknowledge those individuals, human and non-human, who have made a lasting impact on who I am today. They took a shy boy and matured him into a man, husband, father, writer, teacher, communicator, and wayshower. That I am a happy man is largely due to their positive influences.

I offer many thanks to my wife Heidi, who has been my companion, lover, and constant support for the years of my maturation.

The following have been, and in many cases continue to be, my mentors and teachers. They appear in chronological order: Earl "Kim" Kimmel, Gerry Kimmel, Elmer Drake, Bee J. Drake, Jerry Heibel, Merle Ackerman, Jack Savidge, John Boyle, Tom McGeary, Chet Winter, Paul Haber, Dr. Steven Greer, Justine, Moraine, Bren-Ton, Adrial, Jim Self, Joan Walker, The One, and Archangel Michael. My gratitude to each of them, for they have greatly helped me along my journey.

There have been a number of other people who have come into my life. These have provided significant challenges from which I have learned much. My thanks to each of them.

I wish to thank those who have helped with the preparation of this book. I have had support and editing critique from several special friends, both human and non-physical. I honor the fine work that Annie Miller has done in converting my manuscript into the book you have before you, plus the design of its cover.

It has been my great privilege to work on this book in conjunction with many non-humans. I am most grateful for their support, their insights, and their words as we joined together to create the finished product.

Chrysalis

Mark Kimmel

Mark has spoken at international forums, been a guest on radio and television shows, and has conducted workshops based on his unique insights into the transformation of Earth and her humans. Mark's books, *Trillion, Decimal, One, Birthing A New Civilization*, and *Transformation*, contain messages from off-planet sources such as the Andromedans and celestials. His new book, *Chrysalis*, is being written in conjunction with the Archangels.

By focusing on both extraterrestrials and Archangels in his writing and speaking, Mark weaves a credible picture of the larger reality while presenting an uplifting vision for the future of mankind and of our planet. Mark avoids the sensational and fear-riddled perspectives that plague many who deal with the ET phenomena, and the secrecy and misinformation surrounding it, while presenting insights about Archangels without a religious orientation.

Mark moved to his current passion from a successful business career where he had worked for major corporations, then founded and ran three of the most respected Colorado venture capital funds. In addition to providing capital, Mark served on portfolio companies' boards and helped them with strategy and tactics. He retired from business in 1996 to pursue his quest into the larger aspects of our existence. Mark has been listed in *Who's Who* since 1985. He has degrees in engineering, marketing, finance, psychology, and divinity.

Mark is married with two grown sons and four grandchildren. He spends his days writing and speaking about this, the pivotal juncture in human history, and how each person has the power to make this metamorphic transformation positive for all on this planet. He is the founder of the *Cosmic Paradigm Network*, an international group dedicated to manifesting such a transformation.

CONTACT for Mark Kimmel

Email: CP@zqyx.org
Web Site: http://www.cosmicparadigm.com/